REMO WALKS around LAKELAND

by

Graham K. Dugdale

Illustrations by David Macaulay

Westmorland Gazette, Kendal, Cumbria

ISBN 0 902272 78 0

**Published by Westmorland Gazette,
22 Stricklandgate, Kendal, Cumbria LA9 4NE**

Printed by
Dixon Printing Co. Ltd
Burneside Road, Kendal, Cumbria

THE WALKS

All the walks in this volume are numbered according to the degree of effort required from the point of view of a male fell walker of - dare I say it - average fitness. The level of estimated difficulty must inevitably be an arbitrary one, and no doubt readers will arrive at their own conclusions as to its applicability with regard to their own particular circumstances.

Another feature regarding the general distribution of the walks concerns their bias in favour of the eastern half of the region. No haphazard choice I can assure you in view of my north Lancashire base and somewhat ancient means of transportation.

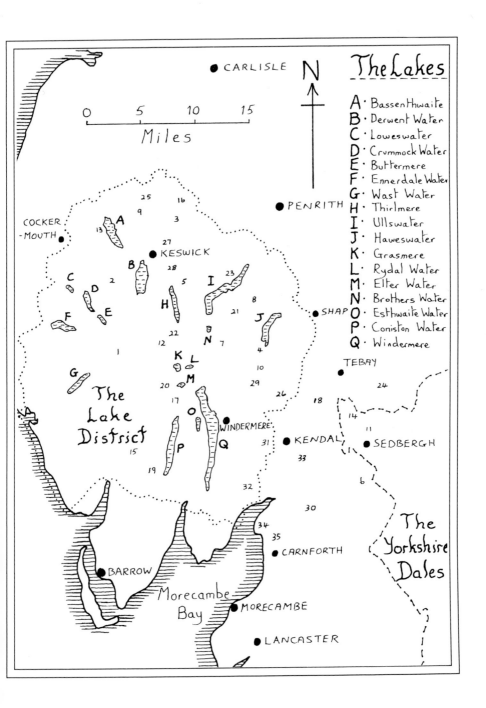

INTRODUCTION

"Not another Lake District guide for walkers!" I hear you mutter with ill-concealed irritation. But wait - this is no ordinary guide to the heartland of a region which has received more attention from writers than any other on the British mainland. The shelves of booksellers are already saturated with an abundance of walking guides. Another of similar content would inevitably suffer an ignominious fate of indifference, vanishing forever into the literary opaque world of the 'also ran'.

In these pages you will find little mention of those magical epithets that have captured the hearts and minds of visitors since the time of that most celebrated of Lakeland residents - William Wordsworth. Names such as Scafell, Gable and Pillar slip off the tongue like a mountain torrent in full spate. All are noble guardians of this classic landscape with more claim to permanent residency that any mere mortal. However, the increasing awareness of the charms and challenges on offer in this most famous of National Parks has led to a degree of over exposure unimaginable even twenty years ago. These once proud sentinels now lie bruised and battered under an onslought of heavily-booted pedestrians.

The days when it was the norm to wander at will along narrow mountain trails, free from unwelcome intrusion into one's personal, rock-girt kingdom, appear to be gone forever. Multitudes of like minded individuals attempting to escape the bustle of city life are causing queues where once the golden eagle ruled supreme. 'Getting away from it all' has lost its meaning on paths that are fast approaching the proportions of multi-lane highways. Only by venturing into the lonely outposts of Lakeland can one come to fully appreciate the true character of the region.

Most of the walks herein described lie on the outer fringe of the district where it is rare indeed to encounter other fell wanderers - unless, of course, they have the good fortune to possess one of these books. Even so, you are more likely to have these fells to yourself for most of the time. I make no apology for adopting a selfish attitude in my desire for privacy as this is one of my reasons for venturing onto the fells. I have no fears that pushing back unknown frontiers will spoil the more remote corners. The vast majority of visitors will always seek out the most spectacular mountains. By introducing readers to the neglected backwaters, I hope to enhance the region's authentic flavour, all too frequently masked by a glossy show of commercialism.

I have no intention of dispensing a deluge of fell-walking advice that I myself have been frequently seen to ignore. Those who have the eminent good sense to purchase this immortal volume will, I am sure, realise the need for adequate preparation. Many of the walks you will soon have the pleasure of sampling venture into what can only be described loosely as virgin territory. The paths that cross these lonely fells are often sketchy and frequently disappear altogether. Consequently, you are strongly recommended to acquire the maps suggested at the start of each walk together with a suitable compass in order to ensure a safe return to your starting point. Please make certain that you are competent in the use of these vital instruments. The unearthly feeling of not quite knowing where you are in a thick fell mist is one that you could well do without.

As the vast majority of walkers are more than likely to make use of a car, the walks have been arranged in a circular manner, starting and finishing at the same point. In these times of ever-decreasing cut backs in rural public transport, one's own motor vehicle must be regarded as a necessity. Indeed, many of the valleys are well off the beaten track and could not otherwise be visited without such assistance.

Walking in an upland area encompasses a wide variety of scenery and must inevitably involve a certain amount of upward perambulation. This of course is its main attraction and although the valleys possess their own inherent charms, my personal preference is for the heights above. Consequently, all walks in this book have at least one fell summit as their prime objective. Nothing can surpass the feeling of elation one achieves upon attaining the summit cairn. This hallowed ground is lord over all it surveys and deserves more than just a passing glance. So linger awhile and savour the panoramic vista that will almost certainly open up before you - weather permitting, naturally.

All the walks take advantage of existing footpaths noted on the official maps as well as some not listed. I personally take great pleasure in following thin upland paths that meander across an ever-changing landscape and find this infinitely preferable to blundering drunkenly over ankle-jarring moorland.

Inevitably some routes do lie across pathless terrain where human activity is a distinct rarity. Where this occurs, directions are given in the appropriate route description.

None of these walks should present any problems with regard to the crossing of private land. Where this does occur, officially approved footpaths and rights-of-way are made use of. Few restrictions are placed on the movement of people across open fell country. Nevertheless, all barriers must be respected and are only negotiated using gates, stiles and established gaps erected for such use. All route descriptions were accurate at the time of writing but guarantees as to the future condition concerning through movement cannot obviously be given. You would be unlucky indeed to be so obstructed but, all the same, the warning must be given.

Another more serious problem concerns the behaviour of man's best friend. Dogs must be kept under strict control at all times, particularly in the lambing season. Too many newly born lambs are lost each year because of dogs which lack proper fell training.

If you enjoy the walks outlined in this book as much as I did then my aim in writing it will have been achieved. Happy hiking!

Graham K. Dugdale

KEY TO MAPS

A 590 Main Roads

⚊ **B5634** Secondary Roads

⚊ Minor Roads

⚊ Narrow Lanes

╫╫╫╫╫ Railway Lines

- - - - Main Fell Paths

⇶ → ~ Route to be followed

⌇ Water courses

◯ Lakes & Tarns

Marshy ground

Coniferous Woodland

Deciduous Woodland

Mixed Woodland

Steep Crags

Ravines

▲ Main Summits

△ Other Prominent Heights & cairns

· Spot Heights

·········· Important Walls

╂╂╂╂╂╂ Important Fences

P Parking for cars

■ Buildings

⋈ Bridges

National Park Limits

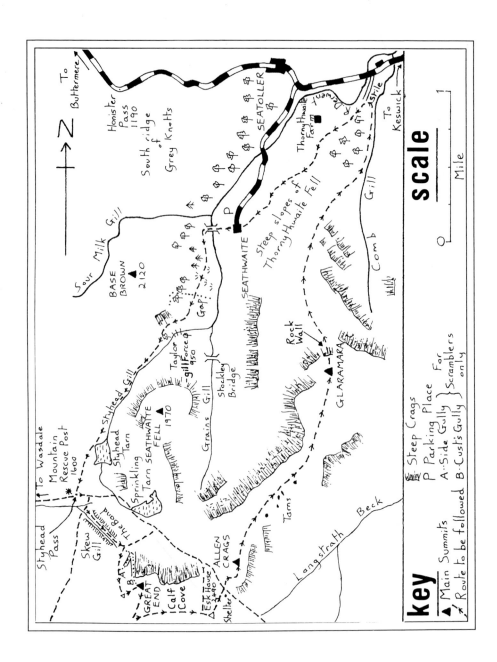

key

▲ Main Summits
P Parking Place
🌿🌿🌿 Steep Crags
🔆🌟 Route to be followed

For
Scramblers
only

A - Side Gully
B - Cust's Gully

scale

0 ——————— 1 Mile

↑ N   To Buttermere

1. GREAT END SCRAMBLE

Start and Finish: Space for cars to park is available where the road ends at Seathwaite, a farming hamlet at the head of Borrowdale.

Summits Visited:	Great End	-2984 feet
	Allen Crags	-2572 feet
	Glaramara	-2560 feet

Total Height Climbed: 3,400 feet

Distance Walked: 9.5 miles

Nearest Centre: Seatoller

Maps Required: Ordnance Survey English Lakes 1:25000, North West and South West area sheets

INTRODUCTION

For those who love the feel of solid rock beneath their boots and enjoy getting to grips with the fells, this walk is among the best. Although of particular interest to bold individuals who actively seek out the most adventurous route to the heights, ordinary walkers should not be discouraged. Ample provision is made for them.

Two major mountain passes are complemented by gully scrambling in the most spectacular and rugged scenery. Dominating its surroundings, Great End presents a solid, unyielding frontage when approached from Borrowdale. The southern aspect, commanded by Scafell Pike, gives no hint of this awesome power. The mountain is frequently overlooked as being of little worth by those hurrying to visit big brother along the ridge, a misconception fully rectified on this walk.

Who could fail to be stirred by an emotive sense of awareness on the final approach to this premier climbing ground? The magnetic presence of such monolithic titans is an irresistible draw to the many who crave the physical contact of hard rock hiking. By taking advantage of the route herein suggested however, the bulk of these intruders should be avoided.

ROUTE DESCRIPTION

On the day I arrived, the farming hamlet of Seathwaite certainly lived up to its unenviable reputation as the wettest inhabited place in Britain. Nevertheless, with suitable waterproofs and the eternal optimism essential to every hill walker, I took the path through the archway in the farmyard. Across the footbridge, a left turn through a gated stile encounters a quiet path alongside the River Derwent - relatively traffic free compared with the popular Stockley Bridge route. After passing the small plantation, the path on your right slants across the open fellside improving after a marshy start, passing through a wall gap en route.

Where the path swings right into the confines of the lower section of Styhead Gill, the opportunity to sample some easy rock scrambling can be enjoyed. The rocky path steepens appreciably as it accompanies the precipitous east face of Base Brown. The requisite muscle stretching and knee bending provides excellent practice for better things to come. At the same time, admire the spectacular waterfall of Taylorgill Force immediately ahead. Its impressive plunge is considerably enhanced after heavy rain - a first class reason for venturing onto the fells in wet weather. At the head of the Force the path encounters a handful of trees before the gradient eases. Continue ahead on the right of Styhead Gill towards the splendid tarn which nestles between towering ramparts.

After reaching the major crossroad at Styhead Pass, turn left towards the impregnable south face of Great End, soon branching right along the 'corridor route' for Scafell Pike. The gaping ravine of Skew Gill beckons to the spirit of adventure in those hardy souls who relish life on the wild side. Ascend the stony bed of the gill sticking close to the stream for the most exciting scramble. Hemmed in by towering rock walls, the only honourable way us upward on all fours. Move left at the head of the ravine to avoid the steep loose scree.

At the col, a short rest is in order to settle one's nerves after this exhilarating climb. Then proceed south up the rocky slope following the path straight up onto the deserted summit of Great End. I attempted to reach the top by way of the steep and narrow Cust's Gully but was forced to retreat for the second time because of deep snow drifts filling much of the gully. This side of the mountain receives little sun and consequently snow lingers well into the summer. That's my excuse anyway.

The shorter side gully forking right near the start of Cust's Gully is another possibility but will no doubt be ridiculed by those heading for the 'real climbing' on Central Gully. We who have tried and failed can always mutter promises about returning when conditions are more favourable before beating an ignominious retreat to follow the walkers' path. Those who prefer the adrenaline to flow in others and wish to avoid the problems and potential dangers of rock scrambling should follow the alternative route indicated on the map by way of Sprinkling Tarn.

From the summit of Great End, follow the narrow path that emerges among the rash of stones down to the depression and join the well-blazed trail to the Pike. Turn aside from it today and head left down into Calf Cove towards the celebrated pass of Esk Hause. This other well known crossroads is unusual in that it lies on two levels which can cause some confusion in mist. Take a left at the higher section and descend 100 feet to the lower pass which is at right angles. Our way lies past the cross wallshelter and up the facing slope onto Allen Crags.

The elongated ridge to Glaramara appears longer than it actually is following a series of switch backs up onto this final rocky eminence. The sweeping descent over Thornythwaite Fell is quite straightforward. It makes use of a good path which takes in a spectacular rock wall close to the summit. Having an abundance of holds, this simple scramble is easy and makes an exhilarating little extra to the descent - don't be tempted to by-pass it.

At the lower end of the north ridge the path accompanies Comb Gill for a short distance before swinging away left towards the Thornythwaite Farm access lane. Take a left here and follow a clear path through the valley fields back to Seathwaite and a well earned cuppa at the farm cafe.

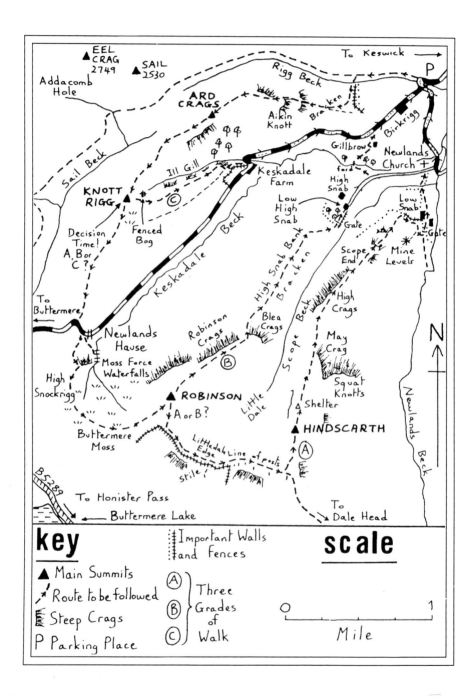

2. KESKADALE RIDGES

Start and Finish: One mile out of Stair along the Buttermere road, a disused quarry provides ample parking space on the right, immediately before a sharp left hand bend where the road crosses Rigg Beck.

Summits Visited:	Ard Crags	-1860 feet
	Knott Rigg(C)	-1790 feet
	Robinson (B)	-2417 feet
	Hindscarth (A)	-2385 feet
Total Height Climbed:	Walk C	-1600 feet
	Walk B	-3000 feet
	Walk A	-3500 feet
Distance Walked:	Walk C	-5 miles
	Walk B	-8.5 miles
	Walk A	-10 miles
Nearest Centre:	Portinscale	

Map Required: Ordnance Survey English Lakes 1:25000, North West area sheet.

INTRODUCTION

For those who relish the satisfying exhilaration to be gained from high level ridge walking, the fells of north west Lakeland are second to none in the district. Nowhere else will you find such profusion of long, narrow ridges dividing deep, glacial troughs and culminating in peaks of character. None of the mountain tops, however, can match the approaches along the network of superbly bladed ridges.

Most of the walks in the area can be completed as horseshoe circuits and I have included a choice of three that can be attempted which should satisfy all walkers, whatever their level of ambition. It must be admitted that the traverse of the main ridges does indeed attract many visitors. That is, apart from a small circuit which has been thankfully overlooked - a dwarf amongst its more extensive neighbours, but no less enjoyable for its lack of physical stature. As a ridge walk it possesses all the essential attributes required from a de-luxe ridge.

All three return phases are along narrow ridges, those descending from Robinson and Hindscarth being very similar in structure, facing one another across the unfrequented valley of Little Dale. Scope End off Hindscarth has the 'edge' however, if you will excuse the pun, and earns full marks as the most rewarding of Class A walks for those willing to put in the extra effort.

Be prepared for numerous encounters which cannot be avoided along the route beyond Buttermere Moss. The badly eroded state of the paths, due mainly to the flaky nature of the underlying slate, is testament to the increased passage of heavy-booted pedestrians. Nevertheless, this is not Great Langdale and queuing up to pay customary tribute to the summit cairn is unheard of.

ROUTE DESCRIPTION

A clear track leaves the quarry car park to follow the right bank of Rigg Beck. Where a fence ascends the opposite bank to cross the lower extremities of the Ard Crags ridge, descend to and ford the beck, following the fence up towards the crest. A thin path forks right through the bracken to join a clearer track heading west up the narrowing ridge of Aiken Knott, the crusty eastern shoulder of Ard Crags.

Progressing through a perfect combination of purple heather and fruit-bearing bilberry couches, one could be forgiven for deciding so early on that Walk C is more than adequate to satisfy your 'inner' needs. I would be the last one to argue against such a decision having myself so determined on a previous visit.

The summit is the highest point along the main arete and is gained in a series of steps, a will-o'-the-wisp until the final approach. On both sides the declevity is precipitous until the ridge broadens as the depression at the head of Ill Gill is crossed on the way to Knott Rigg. Heather gives way to grass as the easy passage is made.

On the top, decide whether to continue, or return to Keskadale down the distinctive east ridge. If the latter is to be followed, head due east across the grassy hollow past a fenced bog. A thin path can be traced down the rim but the obvious way is along the knife edge. Join the main track alongside a fence before descending to the farm. This other track follows a course below the ridge crest and is only to be preferred when the mist is down.

If walks A or B are to be attempted, proceed in a direct south south easterly course across the spongy grass plateau before gaining the more defined ridge route down to Newlands Hause - the road pass to Buttermere. On the easy descent, note the spectacular Moss Force and the two paths leaving the Hause. Avoid the left one which visits the waterfalls. Instead, climb the steep, well-marked path between outcroppings, emerging onto the upper plateau via a narrow rock cutting. This is the terminus for most visitors as the ill-defined continuation of the path testifies.

Bear right to circle the notorious swamp of Buttermere Moss. Keep as high as possible to avoid the worst of the morass, a virtually impossible task. He who escapes with dry feet can indeed depend on his footwear for any occasion. Rising ground to the east brings us to the start of the acclivitous pull onto Robinson. The steep, initial section is badly eroded, the original path having completely disappeared.

It is decision time once again as the rocky summit plateau is reached. Those who have had enough climbing for one day can take the broad north east ridge alongside Robinson Crags. Note the distinct left turn which leads down a series of rock steps along the bracken-covered, narrowing ridge of High Snab Bank. A path escapes right slanting down the steep banking to a wall corner joining the old valley mine road.

After Low High Snab (think about it!), the road to Newlands Church begins. Where the road bears right at the start of a wood, take the path on the left which fords Keskadale Beck and climbs past Gillbrow to the Newlands Road.

Superpersons with kryptonite in their veins should head due south from the summit rocks of Robinson across the plateau towards a fence. The path accompanies the fence down a steep slope and across the connecting bridge of Littledale Edge and up the opposite bank. When the fence turns down towards the Buttermere valley, the path climbs a loose trail accompanied by a line of intermittent posts. At the head of the rise beside a distinctive concrete-based post, turn left along the stony top of Hindscarth.

Beyond the apex a large rock shelter dominates the summit ridge. Heading north down the narrowing ridge is a simple matter on this over-exposed footpath. Beyond May Crag, it cuts a thin line through the heather on the right of the ridge crest. Continuing over Scope End, it descends a convex slope entailing care among the crags at the shoulder terminus. Not even the obvious popularity of this ridge can rob it of a first class recommendation.

Forward progress is arrested where a wall and fence meet. Bear right by the fence towards Low Snab Farm. The path leaves the fence to pass the lower reaches of Goldscope Mine before turning back through a gate by the farm buildings - now doubling as a place of refreshment. Three further gates along the half mile of rough access road bring us to Newlands Church.

Turn right into the lane, heading towards Little Town for 100 yards. Take a left at the junction making your way up to the Newlands road. A right turn at the unusual timber-framed house brings us back to the quarry.

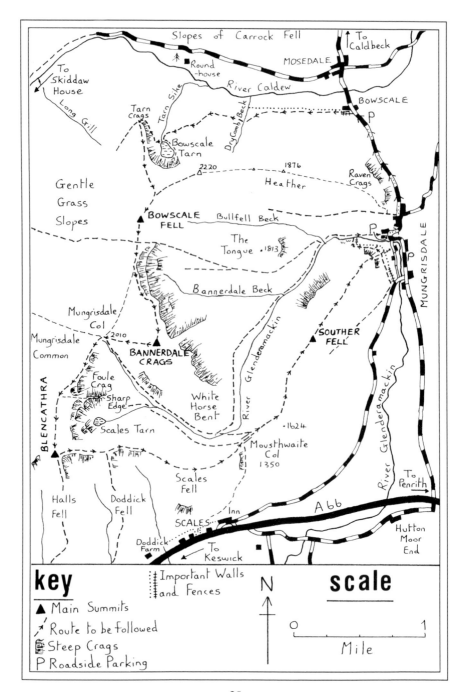

Slopes of Carrock Fell

To Caldbeck

MOSEDALE

To Skiddaw House

Round-house

River Caldew

BOWSCALE

Long Gill

Tarn Sike

Tarn Crags

DryCombe Beck

Bowscale Tarn

Gentle Grass Slopes

2220

1876

Heather

Raven Crags

BOWSCALE FELL

Bullfell Beck

The Tongue •1813

MUNGRISDALE

Bannerdale Beck

Mungrisdale Col

SOUTHER FELL

2010

Mungrisdale Common

BANNERDALE CRAGS

Foule Crag

Sharp Edge

White Horse Bent

River Glenderamackin

BLENCATHRA

Scales Tarn

•1624

Mousthwaite Col 1350

Scales Fell

River Glenderamackin

To Penrith

Halls Fell

Doddick Fell

Inn

A66

SCALES

Hutton Moor End

Doddick Farm

To Keswick

key

⋮ Important Walls and Fences

N

scale

▲ Main Summits

↗ Route to be followed

Steep Crags

P Roadside Parking

0   1

Mile

20

3.   B FOR BLENCATHRA?

Start and Finish: Roadside parking is available in the village of Mungrisdale and on the grass verge approaching Bowscale.

Summits Visited:

Bowscale Fell	-2306 feet
Bannerdale Crags	-2230 feet
Blencathra	-2847 feet
Souther Fell	-1680 feet

Total Height Climbed: 2930 feet

Distance Walked: 10.5 miles

Nearest Centre: Mungrisdale

Map Required: Ordnance Survey Landranger Series1:50000, Penrith, Keswick and Ambleside areas, Sheet No. 90.

INTRODUCTION

I have little hesitation in presenting my award for the most eye-catching colossus in Lakeland to the lyrically titled Blencathra. Like an ancient pterodactyl carousing over its unfortunate prey, this bat-winged titan hovers over his domain, controlling all appproaches.

No fell hunter can remain uninspired nor resist the statuesque challenge of his craggy skeleton.   Unfortunately, it is a fact of life that the most impressive and spectacular landscape features appear to produce their own inevitable magnetism - a Catch 22 situation if ever there was one. A mid week spring visit will definitely help to ease this dilemma - as will the route herein described which gives access to the unfrequented, but no less mouth-watering, fell country to the north.

For those who do not relish the idea of grappling with this land which God gave to Adam, escape is at hand via Mungrisdale Col. A further exit at Mousthwaite Col enables tired limbs to continue their tremulous descent back to Mungrisdale village.

ROUTE DESCRIPTION

Personal preference as to whether the mile of road walking is to be trod at the start or finish of this walk will determine one's parking place. I prefer getting to grips with the fells as early as possible thus electing to park on the wide grass verge approaching the hamlet of Bowscale on the right.

A bridlepath signposted to Bowscale Tarn points the way through a gate. After accompanying a wall as far as Drycomb Beck, the obvious track climbs up towards the tarn at a steady gradient. An abrupt entry is made into the armchair-shaped hollow where Tarn Sike emerges from the corrie. Scooped out by the hand of some glacial sculptor, could he possibly have imagined the artistic legacy of such an obituary?

Crossing the stream, head due west towards the rim of the corrie. The path bends right and gradually climbs a rough, narrow trail to the grassy heights above. Leave the main path, which continues down into the Caldew Valley, turning left to follow the rim up onto the main ridge where a path ascending the east shoulder is joined. Turning right, the man-made shelter on the summit of Bowscale Fell is soon attained.

Circling the glaciated valley head of Bannerdale, the cairn surmounting the Crags is the next objective. The thin path sticks closely to the abrupt, plunging edge and requires careful negotiation in bad conditions. The deep col giving access to Blencathra lies across a pathless grass common a half mile due west of the summit of Bannerdale Crags. The prospect of its ascent can produce a quaking in the stoutest boots. If such is your misfortune, strike south east to follow the River Glenderamackin back to Mungrisdale on a well marked trail.

Looks of wonderous fascination may well be cast towards the knife-edged ridge of Sharp Edge, a classic example of its kind best left to experienced scramblers. Instead, gain the summit crest through the back door by an easy but unremitting toil up the facing slope past the dominating buttress of Foule Crag to the cairn marking the northern point of the 'saddleback' which gives the mountain its alternative name. Blencathra's crowning glory with its unsurpassed southern outlook lies across the shallow depression.

An easy descent down the lip of the east ridge should be taken at a steady pace in order to maintain the splendid exhilaration inherent in high level rock walking. Leave the south-curving arm of Scales Fell to continue down the grass slope and across the perfect saddle of Mousthwaite Col. Ahead, the long grassy shoulder of Souther Fell imbues a deceptive impression of simplicity - another easy summit to be notched up. The immediate pathless flank, however, should not be taken lightly towards the end of this tiring expedition - the Glenderamackin track being easily gained from the col.

If boundless energy - or pride more likely - gains the upper hand, the initial muscle-jarring climb eventually gives way to an easy stroll along the level ridge. A faint path continues over the summit dropping quite steeply to the intake wall above Mungrisdale. Unfortunately, what was until recently a courtesy route across the lower field to the village has now been closed to walkers. A left detour is necessary, passing a lone holly tree, as far as the wall end which enables the River Glenderamackin to be crossed. Gain the valley path up the river bank and turn right back to Mungrisdale. Details of this detour are provided on the larger scale map below.

After Bannerdale Cottage, turn left along the metalled road and follow it back to the car. This mile is soon covered along with the completion of a first rate circuit of these remote fells at the back o'Blencathra.

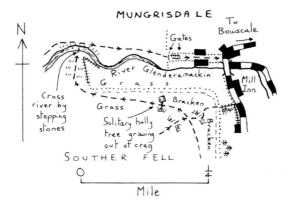

23

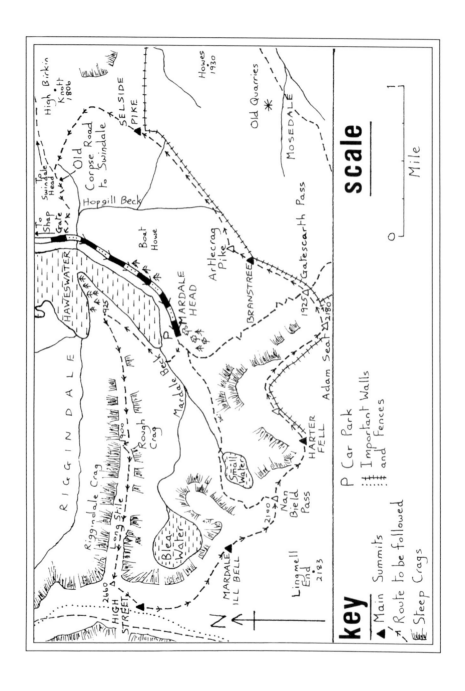

key

▲ Main Summits

/' Route to be followed

⦚ Steep Crags

P Car Park

⫶⫶⫶ Important Walls and Fences

scale

0 ─────── 1

Mile

High Birkin Knott 1806

Howes 1930

SELSIDE PIKE

Old Quarries ✳

MOSEDALE

Old Corpse Road to Swindale

To Swindale Head

Hopgill Beck

To Shap Gate

HAWESWATER

RIGGINDALE

Boat Howe

MARDALE HEAD

Arflecrag Pike

Gatescarth Pass

BRANSTREE

1925

1925 △ 2180

Adam Seat

Riggindale Crag

Long Stile

Rough Crag

1900

Mardale Beck

HARTER FELL

Small Water

Nan Bield Pass

2100

Blea Water

2660

HIGH STREET

MARDALE ILL BELL

Lingmell End 2183

2183

N

24

4. MARDALE HEAD

Start and Finish: The official car park at Mardale Head.

Summits Visited:		
	High Street	-2719 feet
	Mardale Ill Bell	-2496 feet
	Harter Fell	-2539 feet
	Branstree	-2333 feet
	Selside Pike	-2142 feet

Total Height Climbed: 3370 feet

Distance Walked: 10 miles

Nearest Centre: Shap

Map Required: Ordnance Survey English Lakes 1:25000, North East area sheet.

INTRODUCTION

At the head of Haweswater, the road comes to an abrupt end. In this remote corner of Lakeland, nature's wares are laid out in perfect harmony. Those who love to wander in wild and craggy places cannot fail to find here a variety of scenery to suit their taste. The classic sculpturing of Blea Water corrie contrasts sharply with the lonely, pathless fells to the east of Haweswater.

The mountain pass of Nan Bield, linking Mardale and Kentmere, is the most captivating in Lakeland. This sentinel stands guard over Blea Water's smaller, but no less delightful neighbour, Small Water. Take five minutes to ponder awhile and absorb the exhilarating atmosphere that these major crossroads stimulate. Forget the hard sell of contemporary society and cast back in time to the days when laden columns of pack horses wound their tortuous way between the valleys of Lakeland. Today these hallowed places are the preserve of modern day adventurers.

ROUTE DESCRIPTION

Leave the car park at the end of the road and make your way round the head of Haweswater across Mardale Beck. This boggy section is now easily traversed using a series of constructed walkways and bridges. The track turns back alongside the lake towards The Rigg - a wooded promontory overlooking the site of the drowned village of Mardale.

Here, turn sharply up the east ridge accompanying a stone wall towards Rough Crag - a well named obstacle to be negotiated before continuing this excellent line of approach to the summit plateau of High Street. Enjoy the spectacular views on either side of the ridge down to Blea Water and the unfrequented valley of Riggindale before mounting the broken stairway of Long Stile. Once the plateau is reached, head south west to the trig column adjacent to a wall running the full length of the fell - an invaluable guide in bad weather.

The easy walk to Mardale Ill Bell should be a simple stroll around the head of the Blea Water corrie as the objective remains in sight all the way. However, on one occasion during the month of April, I experienced total whiteout conditions on this section of the walk.

Never assume you know the terrain when heavy cloud obscures all landmarks. In such conditions, always have your map and compass to hand for accurate direction finding. A disquieting experience of walking in circles once brought this precept home to me with a vengeance. Lakeland weather can never be taken for granted. Always prepare for the worst by carrying essential equipment for a safe return to base.

From the 'Bell' head off in a south easterly direction aiming for the pass of Nan Bield from whence a superb path picks its way down past the jewel of Small Water. But today, continue up the east ridge onto the domed summit of Harter Fell. When approaching this oddly shaped cairn in mist, one experiences a ghostly feeling of intrusion into some primeval world, soon dispelled by the realisation that it is merely a collection of fence posts.

The walk continues along the extended grassy ridge to the subsidiary summit in a north easterly direction then south east alongside the fence swinging back to the north east and by-passing Adam Seat down to another important crossing point between the valleys of Mardale and Longsleddale - Gatescarth Pass. If time and inclination permit - and they should - instead of heading down to the car park, go straight across and follow the left side of the fence up onto Branstree. This section of the walk is pathless and not recommended in misty conditions.

Striding out on the left of the ridge fence beyond the summit, take a north easterly course for Selside Pike. On this lone journey, the solitary fellwalker can enjoy an exhilarating sense of isolation and remoteness coupled with a humbling awareness of one's privileged position in the open arena of life. Savour this rare opportunity to be alone with nature before rejoining the human race.

The summit cairn of stout proportions lies close to the corner of the fence where it strikes east down towards Mosedale. After descending the north east ridge of Selside Pike, bear left across the marshy depression to join the old corpse-road between Mardale and Swindale. The ghosts of the dead who once passed this way on their last journey to the consecrated graveyard in Shap have long since been laid to rest.

Turn west to follow it down an increasingly declevitous trail of zig-zags on the right of Rowantreethwaite Beck to the valley floor. Passing through a gate to gain the road, turn left for the short walk back to the car park at Mardale Head, a mile distant.

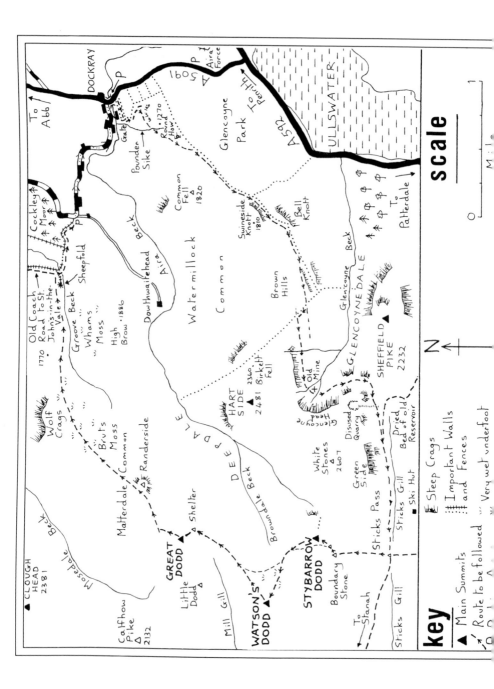

key

▲ Main Summits

▲ Route to be followed

⋯⋯ Very wet underfoot

🗻 Steep Crags

▦ Important Walls and Fences

scale

0   1

Mile

N

5. THE DODDS

Start and Finish: Plenty of room is available on the grass verge which lies 50 yards south of Aira Beck bridge on the right in the hamlet of Dockray.

Summits Visited:	Stybarrow Dodd	-2770 feet
	Watson's Dodd	-2584 feet
	Great Dodd	-2807 feet

Total Height Climbed: 2450 feet

Distance Walked: 11.50 miles

Nearest Centre: Glenridding

Map Required: Ordnance Survey English Lakes 1:25000, North East area sheet.

INTRODUCTION

The elongated ridge of high fells stretching from Grisedale Tarn in the south to the Vale of Keswick in the north, forms an unbroken wall separating the valleys of Patterdale and Thirlmere. Maintaining an altitude that never falls below 2400 feet, this 10 mile promenade has become a classic. For those who revel in the exhilaration of continuous mountain hopping, this unique ridge offers the only one of its kind in the Lake District.

Generally known as the Helvellyn Range, the ridge tops the mesmeric 3000 feet around this most eminent of mountain peaks. Its magnetism is such that visitors are attracted like bees to a honey pot. The finest approach, via the knife-edged ridge of Striding Edge, is a route extolled by every Lakeland writer and one that should be experienced by all who love these hallowed places - but not on this occasion.

The lowest point on the ridge is the crossroads of Sticks Pass; once a well utilised pack horse trail for the region's natural resources, it is now the sole preserve of the modern fell trecker. The gargantuan, ice-carved corries in the south give way to a more undulating landscape composing smooth grass slopes of desolate moorland to the north of the pass.

The traverse of this barren region attracts few visitors yet provides excellent walking with steady gradients throughout. A considerable amount of height is gained with surprisingly few rest stops required, except to admire the ever-improving panorama.

ROUTE DESCRIPTION

Take the rough-walled lane on the left of the A5091 just before the Aira Beck bridge. A gate gives access to the open, verdant pastures of Watermillock Common. Immediately head left, following the wall for a quarter mile before gaining a path that can be clearly seen heading west around the lower slopes of Round How. Cross Pounder Sike and make your way south west on an improving path slanting up the grassy slopes of Common Fell to join the ridge wall. Low outcroppings relieve the monotony of the easy gradients.

The path accompanies the wall around the upper reaches of Glencoyne Park into the magnificent U-shaped valley of Glencoynedale. When the wall begins to descend under Brown Hills, the path continues ahead maintaining a level course until a cross valley wall is reached.

Do not be tempted to stick with this path which loses height steadily. Instead, follow the wall uphill until the miners' path is gained. This ancient thoroughfare contours around the head of the valley on a charming, high-level route above an old mine.   What never ceases to amaze me is how modern man has deliberately sought out these remote isolated outposts merely to gratify his pleasure, whilst his forebears did so for a living and to survive.

The rocky trail climbs gradually across the crumbling buttresses of Glencoyne Head, every step an exquisite delight, and around the east shoulder of White Stones above Nick Head.   A confusing array of old quarry workings makes this untidy amphitheatre a rather ugly corner of the district that is uninspiring and not likely to be remembered with affection - if such is possible in Lakeland.   A descent of about 200 feet across the spoil tip of a yawning quarry hole is necessary to gain the main path.   Make use of the original miners' track, slightly higher than the new one which, although now out of use, is still detectable underfoot.

After rejoining the main path, an increasingly acclivitous ascent on the right bank of Sticks Gill brings us to the small cairned crossroads of the pass. Having gained the main ridge, turn right and follow a thin path up the grass slope onto the lower twin-cairned summit of Stybarrow Dodd.   The main summit can be seen a quarter mile to the north east but, for some obscure reason, the path avoids the highest point.   It is but a slight detour requiring no extra effort to include the upper cairn and rejoin the ridge path.   A short east -facing section of walling provides a useful shelter   to partake of lunch.

Watson's Dodd is easily reached across a shallow, rather marshy depression.   A thin grass path forks left and leads directly to the crowning glory of this otherwise undistinguished probosis jutting out from the ridge. The main path circles the head of Browndale Beck.   Few people bother to visit 'Old Watty', obviously not realising its celebrated status as a recognised Lakeland peak - an understandable error when approaching from the east.

A straightforward walk to the north east regains the ridge track which continues ahead up onto Great Dodd.   The large shelter is often mistaken for the summit which lies a further 100 yards to the north west.   Clough Head, at the terminus of the range, lies another two miles distant - grass all the way broken only by the unusual outcropping of Calf How Pike.   But that must he held in abeyance for another day.

On this occasion, descend the north shoulder until a thin yet consistent path is located heading for Randerside. This rash of stony outcroppings is a welcome oasis amidst the open desolation of Matterdale Common. The long, eliptical perambulation is a lonely yet enjoyable stroll, even across Brunts Moss which must rank as one of the wettest half miles in Lakeland. The path closes with the left bank of Groove Beck as the old coach-road is approached.

Turning right, follow it round past Cockley Moor forestry plantation to the car park at the Dowthwaitehead road junction. Continue east down the road leading back to Dockray. A right at its junction with the A5091 in the centre of the hamlet will bring you back to the car.

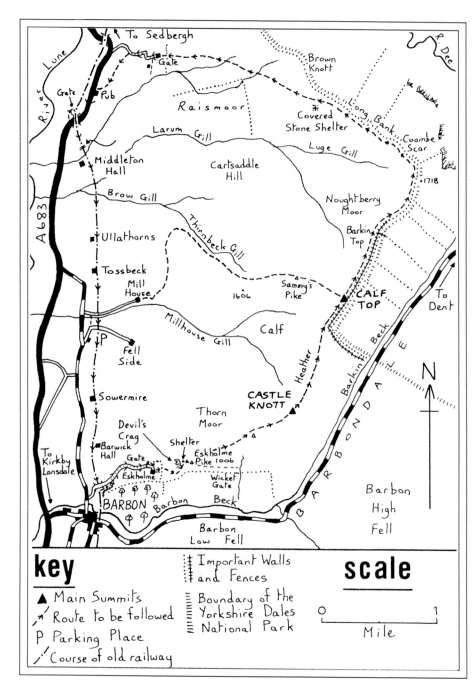

key

▲ Main Summits

↗ Route to be followed

P Parking Place

⌁ Course of old railway

⋮⋮ Important Walls and Fences

☰ Boundary of the Yorkshire Dales National Park

scale

0   1

Mile

River Lune

To Sedbergh

Gate

Gate

Pub

Raismoor

Brown Knott

R. Dee

Long Bank

Covered Stone Shelter

Coombe Scar

Larum Grill

Luge Grill

Middleton Hall

Cartsaddle Hill

Noughberry Moor

•1718

A683

Brow Gill

Thinbeck Gill

Barkin Top

Ullathorns

Tossbeck

Mill House

1606

Sammy's Pike

CALF TOP

To Dent

Millhouse Gill

Calf

Barkin Beck

BARBONDALE

N

Fell Side

Heather

CASTLE KNOTT

Sowermire

Thorn Moor

To Kirkby Lonsdale

Devil's Crag

Barwick Hall

Gate

Shelter

Eskholme Pike 1006

Wicket Gate

Barbon High Fell

Eskholme

BARBON

Barbon Beck

Barbon Low Fell

6. MIDDLETON FELL

Start and Finish: Parking is available where the single file access lane to Fell Side crosses the course of the old railway - grid reference 629852.

Summits Visited:

	Castle Knott	-1759 feet
	Calf Top	-1999 feet

Total Height Climbed: 1850 feet

Distance Walked: 12 miles

Nearest Centre: Kirkby Lonsdale

Map Required: Ordnance Survey Pathfinder Series 1:25000, Middleton Fell, Sheet No. SD 68/78.

INTRODUCTION

The heather-clad triangular wedge of Middleton Fell forms a vast moorland wilderness that has so far been overlooked in the growing upsurge in outdoor pursuits. Sandwiched between the valley of the River Lune and Barbondale, the fell has the appearance of a giant hand dipping its stubby fingers into the chattering surge of this renowned watercourse. The sweeping conchoidal ridge forms a sectional boundary of the Yorkshire Dales National Park and is denied official mountain status only by the height of a single boot. This should in no way undervalue the respect that should be paid to Middleton Fell.

The way is long and should not be undertaken lightly if the full circuit is to be completed and, more importantly, enjoyed. Choose a clear day as paths are faint and rocky landmarks few, particularly on the lower slopes.

The start and finish of the walk follows the course of an old railway track, now abandoned and given over to local farmers for stock grazing. The land is still owned by British Rail, however, and walkers are quite at liberty to make use of it.

The positive, friendly attitude of the local farming community with regard to the use of the trackway by the public is to be commended - special thanks go to Frank Westbury of Tossbeck Farm for his assistance. Readers who take advantage of this man-made highway are asked to respect the numerous fences erected to prevent animals from straying. A detailed analysis of the hazards to be encounterd along this section at the beginning and end of the walk are illustrated on the enlarged map extract opposite.

ROUTE DESCRIPTION

Follow the old railway due south for one and a third miles passing beneath two bridges. Immediately after the second bridge, climb left up the embankment to cross a hurdle. The lane is easily reached twenty yards ahead between a hedge and fence over another hurdle. Turn right along the access road to Eskholme.

A gate at the rear of the farmyard gives access to the pathless right-of-way which accompanies a collapsed wall to a gate in the final in-take wall. Climb this obstacle to gain the open fell - one of many such impediments along the way, all of them contributing to the remote aura of this walk.

There are no paths until the ridge proper above Eskholme Pike is reached. This phase encompasses the steepest ground and the only crag to be encountered on the walk. For this reason an oblique ascent is recommended to ease the acclivity and give the opportunity of visiting Devil's Crag. What appears to be a neat shooting butt and shelter is to be found surmounting this small outcrop.

A path appears in the grass beyond the cairn on Eskholme Pike. Bear left away from the wall to accompany the broad ridge eastwards across Thorn Moor and up towards Castle Knott. The large cairn is a welcome contrast amidst the greenness of the grassy void.

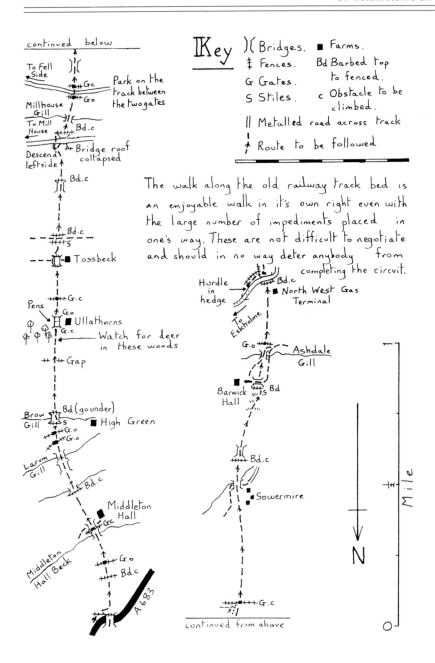

Key

)(Bridges. ■ Farms.

‡ Fences. Bd Barbed top
G Gates. to fenced.
S Stiles. c Obstacle to be
climbed.

‖ Metalled road across track

↑ Route to be followed

The walk along the old railway track bed is an enjoyable walk in it's own right even with the large number of impediments placed in one's way. These are not difficult to negotiate and should in no way deter anybody from completing the circuit.

continued below

To Fell Side
Millhouse Gill
To Mill House
Descend left side ↑
Bridge roof collapsed

Bd.c

Park on the track between the two gates

Bd.c

Bd.c
S

■ Tossbeck

G.c
Pens
G.o
■ Ullathorns
G.c
Watch for deer in these woods

Gap

Brow Gill
Bd (go under)
■ High Green
G.o
G.o
Larum Gill

Bd.c

Middleton Hall
G.c

Middleton Hall Beck
G.o
Bd.c

A 683

Hurdle in hedge
Bd.c
■ North West Gas Terminal
To Eskholme

G.o
Ashdale Gill

Barwick Hall
S Bd

Bd.c

■ Sowermire

G.c
S

continued from above

Mile

N

1

0

Across the wide heathery depression to the north east the highest point on the ridge can be clearly seen. An intermittent track points the way. Make for the boundary fence/wall that leads unerringly to the trig column on Calf Top.

For those who do not relish the continuation of the long, curving, ridge walk, an escape is at hand. Turn west from the summit along the heathery crest of a branching finger pointing to Mill House in the valley. Call at the distinctive cairn on Sammy's Pike (my son claims it as a memorial to his pet hamster) before joining a fell track that meanders down to the farm.

Other more robust individuals, with feet to match, should carry on alongside the wall which bears left around Noughtberry Moor atop Long Bank. The distinct fell track leaves its protective guidance close to an unusual covered rock shelter known as Robin Hurrock Pile - surely not a north country cousin of that illustrious Sherwood outlaw? Stick with this track down to Fell Side. Branch left off the metalled farm road after a quarter mile to follow a short grass path down to the pub on the main road.

Turn south following the A683 towards Kirkby Lonsdale for a half mile until you arrive at a bridge spanning a sharp kink in the road. Make your way up the left banking to gain the old railway track and follow it back to the car using the enlarged map section to assist you.

On my first visit, the main hazard on this final section, apart from barbed prongs in one's hind quarters, was an electric cow barrier soon after the road bridge. I was able to leap over, stride across and crawl under this shocking obstacle putting a sparkle into my step. On a second visit, this booby trap had been removed but nevertheless, the warning must be given in the event of its surreptitous return.

As a second rate alternative, the road walk back to the car is quite straightforward and only slightly further in distance. What a terrific walk this was, with not a soul encountered, and that on a fine bank holiday weekend when, according to press reports, well-known beauty spots were choked with traffic.

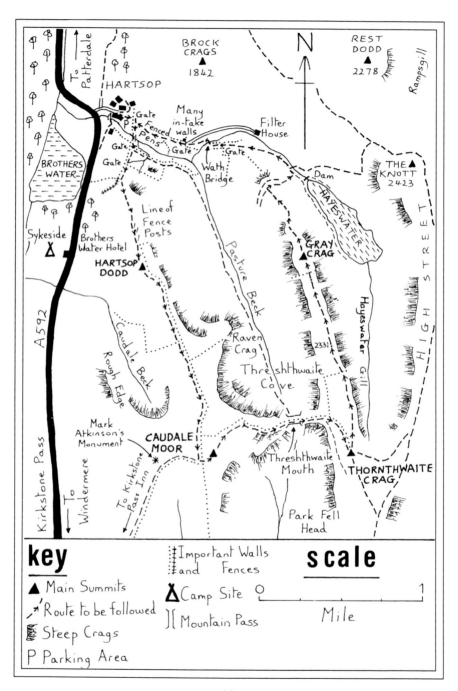

key

▲ Main Summits

↗ Route to be followed

Steep Crags

P Parking Area

⋮ Important Walls
⋮ and Fences

△ Camp Site

][Mountain Pass

scale

0 _____ 1

Mile

7. ABOVE HARTSOP

Start and Finish: A parking area is provided on the east side of Hartsop after negotiating the rough main street which meanders through this picturesque hamlet.

Summits Visited:		
	Hartsop Dodd	-2018 feet
	Caudale Moor	-2502 feet
	Thornthwaite Crag	-2569 feet
	Gray Crag	-2286 feet

Total Height Climbed: 2870 feet

Distance Walked: 7.5 miles

Nearest Centre: Patterdale

Map Required: Ordnance Survey English Lakes 1:25000, North East area sheet.

INTRODUCTION

Descending the scree-choked upper reaches of Kirkstone Pass, the background is dominated by the classic proportions of a magnificent glacially-carved valley. Ullswater and her attendant guardians provide an obvious attraction for the numerous visitors.

Hidden from casual view immediately beyond the squat expanse of Brothers Water, the old world settlement of Hartsop remains a relic of Lakeland's past heritage. Undisturbed by the passage of time and through traffic the hamlet encapsulates all that is best in the district, providing a first class approach to a walk of equal merit.

Once through the unmade street of traditional cottages, however, one is faced with an array of signposted orders that quickly bring you back to the present. Although we should always respect the wishes of permanent residents in the area, these unfortunate reminders will always be an anathema to those of us who seek only to gain the heights above relying on our own initiative and, of course, the relevant O.S. map.

After what had been the wettest June on record, this assault on the fells was planned with just such a pessimistic eventuality in mind. I was not to be disappointed; nor was I worried about getting lost. The key to a safe and enjoyable circuit around Threshthwaite Glen lies in the layout of the ridge walls. Having admirably served successive farmers for more than two centuries, these stoic guides, even though in a collapsing state, have an essential task to perform for today's intrepid fellwalker.

A minimal amount of compass work is needed when the cloud base is well down. The linear orientation along the two broad ridges of Hartsop Dodd and Gray Crag should present no problems to anyone who enjoys a simple yet satisfying challenge. These two main ridges are relatively unfrequented, the majority of walkers being attracted to the superb beacon of Thornthwaite Crag, the most impressive obelisk of any summit in Lakeland

ROUTE DESCRIPTION

After passing through the gate on the east side of the car park, fork immediately right down a clear track which crosses Pasture Beck using a sturdy wooden bridge. Push ahead keeping the wall on your right until the first open field is reached. Here, the main track to Threshthwaite Glen follows a level course eastwards before contouring south into this enclosed valley. Our route lies straight ahead up the field alongside the boundary wall - no path. A gate at the upper edge of the field provides access to the open fell.

A slow but steady plod is required for the ascent up this north arm of Hartsop Dodd. Not quite a 'VS grade' rock climb, it is nevertheless a stiff pull, especially in full waterproofs which hamper one's progress.

Eventually you will arrive at the shoulder blade of the ridge proper where the wall and a new fence plunge down the opposite slope to Brothers Water.

On a strengthening path, continue south south east maintaining whatever gait best suits your upward progression. A line of old fence posts indicates the approach of easier ground. The wall following the crest of the summit ridge is a sure guide to the highest point, a cairn of manly proportions marking this rather obscure station.

The wall is an infallible companion which rises gradually onto Caudale Moor, one old wall being crossed along the way. Keep to the main wall until it turns sharply to the right on the flat plateau. From the wall corner, it is less than 100 yards in a north easterly direction to the summit cairn assigned the over-generous appendage of Stony Cove Pike. A pike is usually conferred on a mountain apex of noble shape and distinction. One would struggle indeed to locate the exact spot across this level tract were it not for the benefit of the suitable rock crown befitting a summit above (just) 2500 feet.

Continue north east to locate another useful wall and path which descend a steep and craggy trail to the fine mountain col of Threshthwaite Mouth. In misty conditions, one is unable to appreciate the awesome grandeur of this truly magnificent crossing point. The verdant slopes along the symmetrical ridges at the two extremities of this walk contrast markedly with this rough mid-section of scrambling which requires careful handling on both sides of the pass.

The steep climb up the opposite bank continues to follow the wall right round to Thornthwaite Crag. This side is composed of much loose scree rather than stepped rock as on the Caudale flank. When the gradient eases, beware of a good path bearing right away from the wall's comforting presence. This by-passes the summit and in mist can lead to all manner of head-scratching dilemmas. Keep firmly to the wall which leads unerringly to the beacon.

The final traverse to Gray Crag should commence on the east of the summit wall. Return along this side for about 50 yards until it bears left to be swallowed by Threshthwaite Mouth. Continue ahead due north avoiding any tendency towards steep ground. A thin path should be picked up and the bearing will gradually ease round to the north north west. After crossing a wall, the ridge narrows with rough steep ground on either flank. The going is easy, however and, in clear weather, a lingering pace should be the order of the day to fully enjoy this traverse along the undulating knife-edge of Gray Crag. Just beyond a second cross fell wall a cairn marks the highest point along the ridge.

The path continues towards the ridge's northern extremity becoming more oblique as the valley of Hayeswater Gill is approached. Beware of a crag hidden from view as one approaches from above. The muscle-jarring descent to the in-take fields can be avoided by turning right at the second of the two sheep trods that contour the fell on this shoulder. The Hayeswater track is easily gained from this point at a higher level.

It is then but an easier and much gentler return to Hartsop. A gate provides access to a walled lane which crosses Wath Bridge and joins the metalled filter house road. Passing through a second gate, the final phase back to the village continues down a fenced passage adjacent to an extensive enclosure of animal pens.

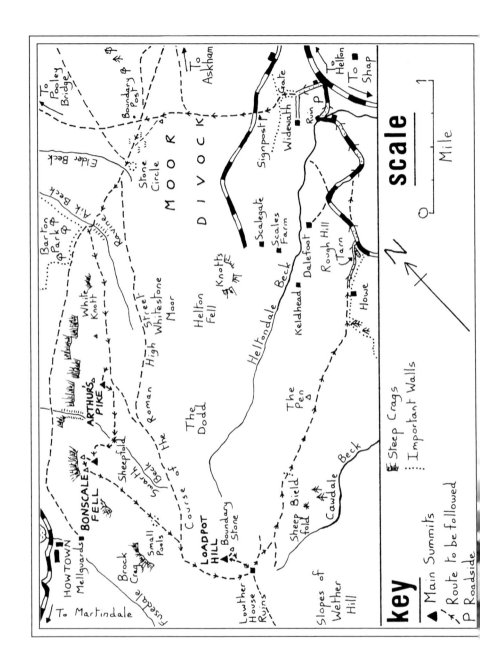

key

▲ Main Summits
↗ Route to be followed
P Roadside
⚡ Steep Crags
⋯⋯ Important Walls

scale

0 ——— Mile 1

N

To Martindale
HOWTOWN
Mellguards
Riesdale
Brock Crag
Small Pools
BONSCALE FELL
Sheepfold
ARTHUR'S PIKE
Swarth Beck
LOADPOT HILL
Boundary Stone
Lowther House Ruins
Sheep Bield fold
Cawdale Beck
Slopes of Wether Hill
The Pen
The Dodd
White Knott
Roman High Street
The Course of
Whitestone Moor
Helton Fell
Knotts
Ravine
Alk Beck
Barton Park
Elder Beck
DIVOCK MOOR
Stone Circle
Boundary Post
To Pooley Bridge
To Askham
Heltondale Beck
Keldhead
Dalefoot
Scales Farm
Scalegate
Signpost P
Widewath
Gate
Run P
To Helton
To Shap
Rough Hill Tarn
Howe

46

8. AROUND HELTONDALE

Start and Finish: From Shap take the road through Bampton that follows the west side of Lowther Valley. A half mile south of Helton, turn left at the first arm of a two lane junction. A roadside pull-in provides limited parking 100 yards down on the right.

Summits Visited:		
	Arthur's Pike	-1747 feet
	Bonscale Pike	-1718 feet
	Loadpot Hill	-2201 feet

Total Height Climbed: 1720 feet

Distance Walked: 11.5 miles

Nearest Centre: Helton

Map Required: Ordnance Survey English Lakes 1:25000, North East area sheet.

INTRODUCTION

Historical associations are dominant within the area encompassed by this walk more than any other I have come across in my travels over the fells. The antiquarian enthusiast will find much to savour among the remnants of early man's involvement with Moor Divock in particular. Tumuli and ancient structures abound in profusion.

The eastern extremity of High Street, constructed by the Romans stationed at Ambleside, makes its final declivity over the moorland wilderness of Loadpot Hill before heading across the lowland pastures to Penrith. Now little more than a grassy rut, one can still empathise with the marching legions who passed this way in times long since consigned to the history books.

A shooting lodge of more recent construction on the south side of the summit has now fallen into ruins and bears little resemblance to its former glory. The aristocratic residents of Lowther Hall would no doubt have appreciated the protection it afforded them from the vagaries of Lakeland's fickle weather.

Those dreamers among us who appreciate visual reminders to stimulate our retrospective appetites, will find much to satisfy this craving around Heltondale. The desolate nature of the landscape adds further to an awe-inspiring sense of antiquity. Twentieth century man, preferring the comforts of contemporary civilisation, is a rare visitor to the Moor, unlike you dear reader who, I hope, will actively seek it out. Like the fell ponies who frequent the upper slopes, we also have an inherent desire to wander in loney places.

ROUTE DESCRIPTION

Return to the main road and take the farm road to Widewath. Where it turns sharply to the left, continue ahead along a rough walled track until a gate is reached giving access to the open moor.

A signpost on the near horizon indicates the direction to take. Crossing the fell road, follow the grass track over Moor Divock in a north westerly direction towards Pateley Bridge. In misty conditions, this extensive plain of bracken and marsh is definitely not the place to lose one's way. The use of map and compass becomes a vital skill, essential for survival in this wild tract.

At a major crossroads close to a boundary post, turn left negotiating a swampy bog to reach an important stone circle. A brief period of silent meditation will rekindle the images of ancient primitive rites performed within the confines of this prehistoric relic.

Continue across Elder Beck towards the deep gash of Aik Beck ravine. A grass track makes a steady direct ascent up the broad north east ridge of Arthur's Pike. A stony cap perched jauntily on the protruding dome can be seen at a distance and, although set apart from the main path, is easily gained by a short detour. Rising but little above the surrounding fell, few will realise the abrupt plunge of the north west face down to the placid waters of Ullswater.

Bonscale Pike displays a rather prosaic appearance from this angle, gentle, grassy slopes deterring exploration by all save the avid peak-bagger and guide book writer. Join a good path heading south west towards a sheepfold in the dividing valley of Swarth Beck. Crossing the beck, it is a short, easy ascent onto the summit - an unpretentious mound that appears at first sight to be hardly worth the effort of its attainment. A visit to the proud beacons teetering on the edge of the steeply shelving ramparts will, however, soon disperse any misgivings.

Heading due south across the broad grass plateau, pick up a narrow trod that leads past a scattering of pools and up to join the High Street track. Go right to circle the upper slopes of Loadpot Hill bearing left until the remains of Lowther House are reached. A path heads north onto the dual summit comprising a modern trig column and an ancient boundary stone.

After returning to the ruin, follow the obvious path heading east for a short distance only. Leave it to strike down and join the grooved path making its way eastwards past a short bield and over The Pen. Pass to the right of this prominent cairn, isolated atop the broad grassy verdure of this eastern arm of Loadpot Hill, inhabited only by the resident fell ponies and sheep.

A gradual descent brings us to Howe Farm - the first settlement to be encountered on this walk and a testament to its remote nature. The rough farm road joins a metalled highway by Rough Hill Tarn. Head left and follow the zig-zags back to the car.

49

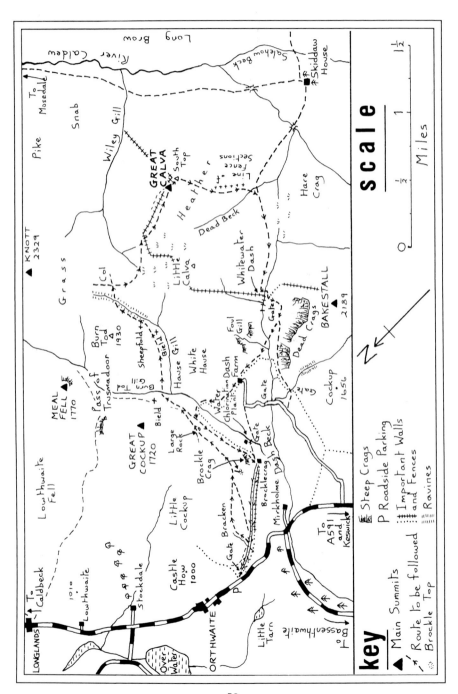

key

▲ Main Summits

🖍 Route to be followed
⋯ Brockle Top

🅿 Roadside Parking

⛰ Steep Crags

✶✶ Important Walls and Fences

⋮⋮ Ravines

scale

0 ½ 1 1½

Miles

50

9. A DASH OF CALVA

Start and Finish: The farm access road signposted to Brocklecrag which starts a quarter mile south of Orthwaite.

Summit Visited: Great Calva   -2265 feet

Total Height Climbed: 1550 feet

Distance Walked: 7.5 miles

Nearest Centre: Bassenthwaite Village

Map Required: Ordnance Survey Landranger Series1:50000, Penrith, Keswick and Ambleside areas, Sheet No. 90.

INTRODUCTION

Those individuals who believe that there is no fell country left in Lakeland where a free spirit can wander alone should cast their scowling gaze to the tops at the 'back o' Skidda'.   On a certain bank holiday weekend, when the valleys and more illustrious heights were teeming with humanity, these rolling uplands remained undisturbed.

Everyone recognises the mountains that make up the glossy facade - Skiddaw and Blencathra, but who has ever heard mention of Great Calva. "And who wants to waste valuable energy on that boring lump" is the usual incogitant reply. Bigots who elicit such pedantic rejoinders have obviously developed little feeling for the authentic spirit of fell walking.

One may legitimately refer to these grass and heather clad uplands as monotonous and desolate, but never boring. This disparaging word should never be uttered in connection with fell walking.

All is not verdant rough grazing, however. The superb ravine of Hause Gill provides an exhilarating route onto the rolling upper slopes on the outward journey. A return by way of Dash Beck introduces the classic scenery of plunging waterfalls and rearing buttresses normally associated with the core of the region.

ROUTE DESCRIPTION

After parking on the roadside pull-in a short distance past the Brocklecrag access road, make your way along this metalled section for no more than 200 yards as far as a wet grassy area on the left. A stream passes under the road here and marks the start of a delightful trail across the lower slopes of Little Cockup. The initial 50 yards is pathless on grass but a thin track soon emerges, the easy gradients a pleasure to tread.

As height is gained, the start of the official bridleway can be seen below indicated by a wooden signpost. The two paths join at the head of a shallow valley, dry in its upper reaches. A groove points the way at the opposite side up onto the short connecting ridge to Brockle Top. This isolated outlier from the main crag provides an excellent viewpoint across the lower pastures of Dash Valley - the grassy sward of the promontory pierced by several quartz-veined teeth of rock.

After leaving this crusty nodule, bear left into the side valley occupied by Hause Gill. The path makes a gradual descent through the bracken to its confluence with Burn Tod Gill, passing a prominent boulder on the way and joining the lower path which traverses below the main bulk of Brockle Crag.

Crossing Burn Tod Gill a little upstream from the confluence, the path continues to follow Hause Gill bearing left past a cross wall bield into the deep cutting of the ravine. Passing a broken sheepfold, the path steepens and interest quickens as progress is made across the exposed vertical banding of brittle Skiddaw slate. All to soon, the end of this super ascent over the oldest rock type in the Lake District is in sight. The path leaves the confines of the ravine, which swings left, and continues ahead up to the grass col.

A distinct path heads left towards the smooth dome of Knott but soon fades as the initial slope steepens in the tough grass. Our route lies to the right following a clear path around the headwaters of Wiley Gill into a squelchy area of heather bog. When the path disappears, continue in a southerly direction until a disintergrating fence is reached.

Cross this near a corner section before picking up the clear path that accompanies the fence onto the splendid pyramid of Great Calva. This distinguished apex is one of the finest in the northern fells boasting its own custom-made shelter. The mountain forms the northern extremity of a huge rift which cleaves the district in two. As well as providing an essential north/south communications link, this elongated trough opens up an unexpectedly distant vistarama. From the immediate foreground of the Glenderaterra Valley south through St. John's-in-the-Vale, Thirlmere and the Vale of Grasmere, one gains the impression of being able to observe south Lakeland through a mountain tunnel.

It is then but a short walk along the summit ridge to the South Top. The dark, heather-clad slopes stretch away in front and must be negotiated to gain the Skiddaw House track. Take a south west course aiming for an emergent path that can be made out a half mile distant. This follows down a series of what appear to be abandoned fire beating impedimenta.

Turn right after joining the old shepherds' track and cross Dash Beck just before it crashes down to the valley bottom in a short yet breathtaking series of silver-flecked cascades. The track follows the left side of the valley under the threatening gaze of Dead Crags.

Leave this track to fork down right, crossing Dash Beck and aiming for the right hand corner of an obvious cross valley wall. The corner is reached soon after Foul Gill and followed past Dash Farm around the west shoulder of White Hause. Stick close to this wall until it crosses Hause Gill. You then join the main path heading south west under the distinctive white splashes of quartz forming Brockle Crag. After meeting the main farm road, a simple stroll back to the Orthwaite road remains.

And so ends a satisfying walk on the finest bank holiday weekend in years, thus proving, once again, that such busy periods do not necessarily have to prohibit those who enjoy the benefits of cloistered walking.

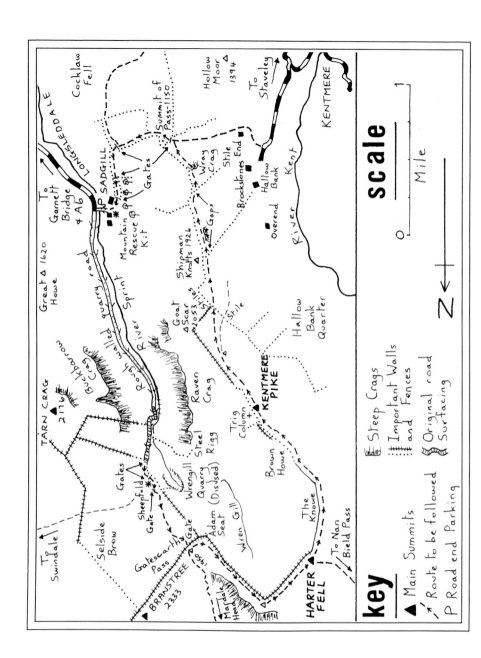

key

▲ Main Summits

↗ Route to be followed

P Road end Parking

▥ Steep Crags

⊹⊹⊹ Important Walls and Fences

〰 Original road Surfacing

scale

0 ——————— 1

Mile

N

Cocklaw Fell

Hollow Moor 1394

To Staveley

Summit of Pass—1150

KENTMERE

To Garnett Bridge & A6

LONGSLEDDALE

P SADGILL

Gates

Mountain Rescue Kit

Great △ 1620 Howe

walled quarry road

River Sprint

Tarn Crag △ 2176

Buckbarrow Crag

To Swindale

Selside Brow

Gates

Gatescarth Pass

Sheepfold

Wren Gill

Wrengill Quarry (Disused)

Steel Rigg

Raven Crag

Rosgill Beck

Goat △ Scar 2053

Stile

Shipman Knotts 1926

Gaps

Wray Crag

Brockstones End

Stile

Hallow Bank

Overend Bank

River Kent

Hallow Bank Quarter

KENTMERE PIKE

Trig Column +

Brown Howe

The Knowe

Adam Seat

Gate

BRANSTREE 2333

To Nan Bield Pass

HARTER FELL

Mardale Head

54

10. LONGSLEDDALE

Start and Finish: Ample parking is available where the Longsleddale road ends at Sadgill.

Summits Visited: Harter Fell   -2539 feet
                          Kentmere Pike -2397 feet

Total Height Climbed: 2150 feet

Distance Walked: 8.5 miles

Nearest Centre: Kendal

Map Required: Ordnance Survey English Lakes 1:25000, South East area sheet.

INTRODUCTION

Five miles north of Kendal along the A6 lies the hidden valley of Longsleddale, the first of a series of eastern dales that receive scant attention in view of their position, remote from the main arteries feeding the National Park. Longsleddale is the last of the 'true' valleys that remain unmistakenly Lakeland in character. Further east, the influence of the Pennine type of landscape assumes a dominant role.

The constricted entrance to the valley is easily missed so keep a sharp lookout for the Longsleddale road sign indicating a narrow lane which first descends to the hamlet of Garnett Bridge. The long approach to reach the end of this road at Sadgill - much of it in third gear - is well worth the effort, if only to marvel at the dramatic contrast in scenery that unfolds. The sylvan greenery of the lower dale gives way to an abrupt cataclysmic display of awesome power.

The finely chiselled rock buttresses of monolithic grandeur compress the youthful River Sprint into a cascading ravine.   Excellent scope for scramblers is available in the gullies and shattered ramparts around Raven and Buckbarrow Crags. This humble soul has no such daring aspirations, however, as this walk illustrates. The ridge separating the parallel valleys of Kentmere and Longsleddale is easily attained and the view sufficient to awaken the spirit of adventure in the most timid breast.

Walls and fences abound in profusion hereabouts acting the part of invaluable guides to the walker who lacks confidence in his map-reading ability. In fact, it is very difficult to go astray in view of their continuous presence.   Like an irritating chaperone, they refuse to be sidetracked, maintaining a firm influence from start to finish. Having walked the ridge from Harter Fell south on numerous occasions, it always appears to be longer than it actually is despite the gentle gradients which encourage a fast pace. I attribute this to the boundary lines along the crest which stretch away towards the fading horizon and emphasise the distance still to be covered.

Those readers who have been avid followers of the walks in this book may have remembered that we visited Harter Fell on Walk No 4: Mardale Head. The section from the summit to Gatescarth Pass is reversed on the present walk, thankfully in clear weather. This is the first occasion that a section of a previous walk has been duplicated, only one other summit being revisited in the book, which isn't bad going really.

Approaching summits from a different direction provides the variety of scenery and experience that retains the route's individuality until the final apex is attained. All mountains possess a range of options to choose from, each with its own character and, therefore, justification for a revisit.

ROUTE DESCRIPTION

The way continues beyond Sadgill as a rough walled road climbing up the right bank of the ravine towards the quarries, all now abandoned and derelict.   At this point, the civil engineering abilities of the early road builders can be seen in the form of a compacted slate surface over which heavily laiden carts once trundled on their way down to the valley.

Pass through a gate where the road ends following the wall round to the left. The bridleway heading north east for Swindale is signposted but difficult to locate. This is not a problem to worry us, however, as we keep to the main track through two more gates abutting a large sheepfold.

Keep the wall on your left until the entrance to Wrengill Quarry is reached, identified by a wire-mesh barrier preventing access. After this, the cairned path zig-zags up the open fell out of Brownhowe Bottom bearing slowly left over easy slopes of grass towards Gatescarth Pass. Immediately after the pass gate, turn left up the steepening grass slope towards the prominence of Adam Seat. The path avoids this boundary marker, joining the fence beyond and following it over Little Harter Fell all the way to the twin cairned summit ridge.

The south west cairn, being imperceptibly higher, marks the zenith of the fell. In clear conditions, the mystic eeriness of this unique edifice is lacking and on this visit presented the appearance of a stranded darlek from the legendary Dr. Who series. All visitors will no doubt have their own personal interpretations of this unusual folly.

Keep with the fence which heads south across the grassy plateau of The Knowe descending into a shallow, peaty depression before rising alongside a wall onto Kentmere Pike. The wall which crosses the exact summit location divides an obscured trig column on the opposite side from the path from an insignificant heap of stones not worthy to grace the crown of a 2000 feet plus mountain.

Descending the gentle grass slopes to the south east, the wall gives way to a fence. The path bears right, away from this boundary, and forks at a cairn. Take the more distinct left branch which heads for a double stile at a corner where the fence and a lower wall meet. If the crusty elevation of Shipman Knotts is to be visited, cross the fence stile and keep to the left side of the ridge wall - but note that there are no convenient stiles or gaps to regain the main path. Otherwise, cross the wall stile and stick with it all the way to the head of the pass linking the two valleys.

The steepest section of the whole walk, and needing some care, follows a meandering yet easily followed trail down the edge of Wren Crag. The lower stages are rather marshy where the path leaves the wall and makes a beeline for the gate at the head of the pass.

Go left through the gate and follow a rough trail down into Longsleddale with a wall on your left. After another gate, the path swings north with the wall on your right. Yet a further gate gives access to a walled section behind the outbuildings of Sadgill Farm. And a final gate returns us to the metalled farm road crossing Sprint Bridge back to the parking area.

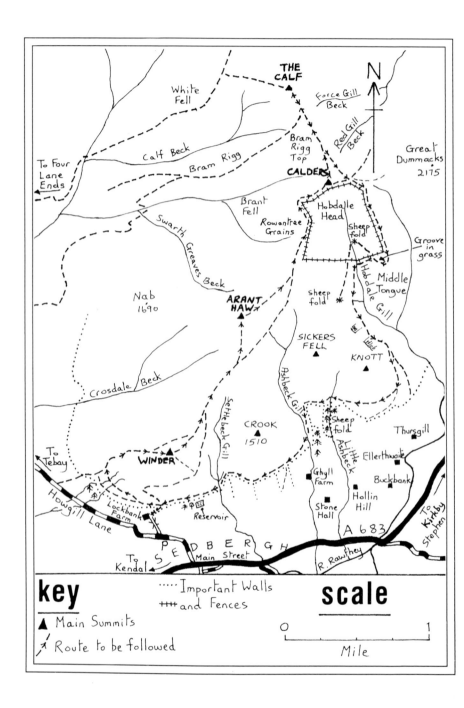

The Calf · White Fell · Force Gill Beck · Calf Beck · Bram Rigg · Bram Rigg Top · Red Gill Beck · Great Dummacks 2175 · To Four Lane Ends · CALDERS · Brant Fell · Hobdale Head · Sheep fold · Groove in grass · Swarth Greaves Beck · Rowantree Grains · Middle Tongue · Nab 1690 · ARANT HAW · Sheep fold · Hobdale Grill · SICKERS FELL · KNOTT · Ashbeck Gill · Crosdale Beck · Settlebeck Gill · CROOK 1510 · Sheep fold · Little Ashbeck · Thursgill · To Tebay · WINDER · Ellerthwaite · Buckbank · Ghyll Farm · Hollin Hill · Stone Hall · To Kirkby Stephen · Howgill Lane · Lockbank Farm · Reservoir · A 683 · SEDBERGH · Main Street · To Kendal · R. Rawthey

key

▲ Main Summits

↗ Route to be followed

····· Important Walls
+++ and Fences

scale

0 ———————— 1

Mile

11. BACK O' SEDBERGH

Start and Finish: Parking is permitted along Howgill Lane on the left close to its junction with Lockbank Farm access road.

Summits Visited:		
	Winder	-1551 feet
	Arant Haw	-1989 feet
	Calders	-2210 feet
	The Calf	-2220 feet

Total Height Climbed:	1750 feet	
	With The Calf	-1950 feet

Distance Walked:	8.5 miles	
	With The Calf	-10.5 miles

Nearest Centre: Sedbergh

Map Required: Ordnance Survey Pathfinder Series 1:25000, Sedbergh and Baugh Fell, Sheet No. SD 69/79.

INTRODUCTION

My original intention on the day I completed this walk was to head for the North Lakeland fells at the back o' Skiddaw. Approaching the Lune Gorge, however, the crystal clarity of the Howgill Fells, etched against a backdrop of brilliant azure, was a temptation impossible to resist. Like icing on a Christmas cake, they beckoned invitingly.

Winter is a season of marked contrasts and on this occasion I was lucky. Views are often much clearer when the land is dusted with a fine mantle of snow emphasising the natural contours of the mountains. Distracting impurities that could mar the scene are filtered out of the icy atmosphere providing a close-up like that seen through a telescope.

For once, the grey blanket was cast aside in favour of a sparkling corona to enhance the surrounding pageantry displayed to perfection. In such conditions one would expect the hills to be ablaze with a myriad of multi-coloured kagools. Such may well be the case in the ever popular Langdale Valley, but not so here. Today the calm serenity of these gentle giants remains unbroken and welcoming.

ROUTE DESCRIPTION

Take the road forking right off Howgill Lane up to Lockbank Farm. A rough walled lane bearing right gives access to the open fell through a gate. Turning left, follow the in-take wall round the lower western slopes of Winder on a distinct path for a half mile until the path fades.

Carry on across a tract of spongy grass to join the main track which ascends the broad west ridge but avoids the highest point. As the gradient eases, a track forking to the right should be followed which brings one to the trig column on the summit of Winder. The temptation to rest awhile should be resisted unless one's climbing aspirations stop here. The circuit of this noble guardian of Sedbergh is a worthy afternoon's stroll in its own right, but today our ambitions lie above and beyond.

The path continues in a north easterly direction towards Arant Haw but once again refuses to acknowledge its presence by skirting east of the summit. Those who wish to pay their respects can easily do so by taking advantage of a path that forks left off the main bridleway to ascend the south ridge. The thin track leads unerringly onto the plateau-like summit where an untidy heap of stones indicates the highest point.

Rejoin the main path by heading north east to accompany a fence down into the broad depression of Rowantree Grains. The track climbs steadily alongside the fence, turning sharp right 150 yards before the summit of Calders. The substantial cairn, adrift on a sea of grass a few yards left of the track, is suitably proportioned in accordance with one's expectations of a 2000 feet mountain.

This is the moment to decide whether a visit the The Calf is to be included in the day's itinerary. Seen across the wide expanse of Bram Rigg Top to the north north west, the detour involves an extra two miles of walking. It is well worth the time and effort to visit the monarch of the Howgills, if you have not already made his acquaintance.

The way is dead straight passing to the east of Bram Rigg Top down to the col separating the headwaters of Calf and Force Gill Becks. It is then but a short uphill stroll to the crown. Retracing your steps, skirt the head of Red Gill Beck bearing left off the main track to Calders and make for the fence. Follow it round to the right then down the arrow-straight ridge of Middle Tongue.

Where the fence turns down into Hobdale, continue ahead for a short distance before bending right to descend into the valley. Take advantage of a distinct groove which slants obliquely down at an easy gradient from left to right. Unfortunately, the fence - which appears to act as a giant sheepfold - obstructs this steady downward progression. A strong temptation to trespass into this enclosure cannot obviously be recommended. The resulting steep descent into Hobdale, although otherwise quite safe, should nevertheless be undertaken with care, preferably in a crablike manner.

Take the time to absorb the remote atmosphere of this superb valley head hidden from casual view and unwelcome intrusion. Follow the lower of the sheep trods which contour out of the valley around the craggy east shoulder of Knott. The west-bound return to Lockbank Farm sticks closely to the north side of the in-take wall all the way. The approach to the side valley of Little Ashbeck is on a fairly steep slope looking down on the wall. Only join this wall after crossing the stream running next to it for a quarter mile. It then turns south at right angles to drop quite abruptly towards a small coniferous plantation. Do not enter this but cross Ashbeck Gill and accompany the wall on a level course along the southern slopes of Crook.

The uphill pull alongside the wall to reach Settlebeck Gill cannot be avoided and is rather a struggle for tired limbs at the end of a long day on the fells. However, once across the stream, the rest of the way is all downhill under the watchful gaze of Winder. At Lockbank Farm, simply reverse the initial outward walk back to Howgill Lane.

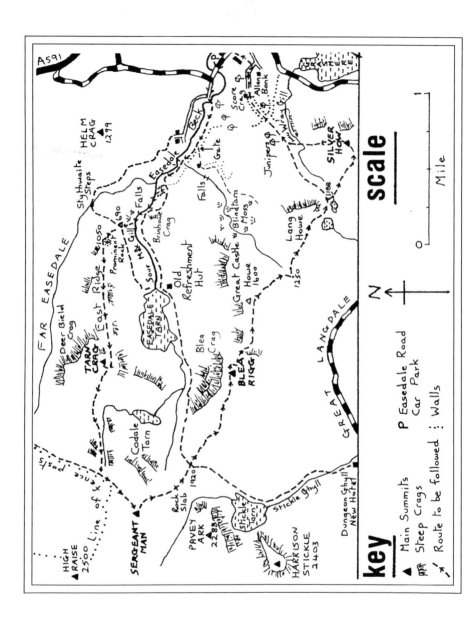

key

▲ Main Summits

🦷 Steep Crags

╱' Route to be followed

P Easedale Road
Car Park

: Walls

scale

N

Mile

12. THE EASEDALE CIRCUIT

Start and Finish: Easedale Road Car Park, Grasmere.

Summits Visited:	Tarn Crag	-1801 feet
	Sergeant Man	-2414 feet
	Blea Rigg	-1776 feet
	Silver How	-1292 feet

Total Height Climbed: 2500 feet

Distance Walked: 9 miles

Nearest Centre: Grasmere

Maps Required: Ordnance Survey English Lakes 1:25000, South East and South West area sheets.

INTRODUCTION

The well trodden path to the hanging valley wherein nestles Easedale Tarn has been a favourite with countless visitors to the charming village of Grasmere for well over a century and remains so today. Although nestling in the heart of Lakeland forming the nucleus of a highly popular region, this walk enables one to quickly escape the merry throngs making their way to the hallowed waters.

The detour from the main path allows for a short yet stimulating scramble among the rocky cascades of Sour Milk Gill. Like its namesake in other parts of the district, this bubbling spout tumbles headlong in its declivitous rush down to the valley floor. Each rivulet, hurrying to outpace its neighbours, creates a silvery web of sparkling threads that twinkle in sunlight.

The principal aim of all the walks in this guide book is to reach the highest point - in this case, the craggy prominence of Sergeant Man.

ROUTE DESCRIPTION

An early start from the car park on Easedale road will avoid the multitudes heading your way. Continue north along the road until the Easedale Tarn signpost indicates the route to be taken. After 200 yards across an open field, the path accompanies a wall on the left with Easedale Beck on the right. Cross Blind Tarn Gill to leave the access track for Brimmer Head Farm, bearing left towards a kissing gate in a cross wall. Go immediately right down a short, walled, grass lane to begin the ascent of Sour Milk Gill.

Route selection can vary considerably and is, therefore, left to individual preference. For those who get hot flushes at the thought of such wild endeavours, the main path should be kept firmly underfoot until the head of the force is reached.

For those more discerning individuals who feel confident of handling simple, bare-rock scrambling between chattering ribbons of foam-flecked milk, this ascent is for you. Always remember that in such hands-on situations, three points of contact with the rock must be maintained at all times. Far too soon, however, this exhilarating diversion is over as the head of the waterfall is gained where Sour Milk Gill squeezes between Brinbow and Ecton Crags.

Keeping to the right side of the stream, bear right to quickly negotiate some marshy ground and locate a thin track that emerges in the bracken. This follows the narrowing east ridge through the bracken heading north west up to a prominent outcrop. From here, tarn gazers can be observed wending their way hopefully towards the old refreshment hut - a futile aim as it is now just a ruin. Only discerning fellwalkers - or the shrewd purchasers of this book - are likely to join you.

An intermittent path becomes more distinct as one progresses up the east ridge. At the final depression, a thin path winds its way up an easy slope to the left of the precipitous buttress upon which the summit cairn resides.

Bearing right at the head of the grass rake, the apex of the crag is approached from behind.

From here, the path meanders in a westerly direction across a peaty common overlooking the hidden gem of Codale Tarn and up a narrow gully. At the head of the gully it meets another path following the old county boundary line up from Far Easedale Head. A left turn takes one directly to the impressive rock pyramid of Sergeant Man - its commanding presence certainly deserving a more meritorious rank. From these craggy ramparts an excellent mountain panorama can be enjoyed in all directions, marred only by the sprawling mass of High Raise to the north.

After descending from this rough pinnacle, the way lies south east down a long, easy ridge on a worn path. Beyond the footpath focus where tracks from Easedale Tarn and Stickle Tarn meet, the Blea Rigg ridge undulates for three quarters of a mile culminating in the rather unpretentious summit eminence. The tortuous path swings south immediately after this nebulous peak and broadens considerably twisting among the numerous outcrops and providing a variety that maintains interest throughout this long descent.

Leave the main track after passing the smaller of the two tarns lying to the south of the prominent crag of Lang How. A thin path here branches right across the grassy plateau. After a gentle climb onto Silver How, one can be excused for lingering awhile to savour the enchanting vista that opens up to the east over Grasmere and Loughrigg. This airy perch at the end of a long day serves merely to emphasise the true interpretation of what 'the good life' really means.

Having satisfied your aesthetic taste buds, take the path heading due north off the summit to cross Wray Gill where it begins to cut deeply into the underlying fellside. Passing through a clump of juniper, the way lies down a rough, overgrown lane which becomes a metalled road at Score Crag Farm. Just before joining Allen Bank's driveway take the faint path which forks left behind a hotel to meet the Easedale road. Turning left, it is but a short stroll back to the car park and the culmination of another memorable day on the fells of Lakeland.

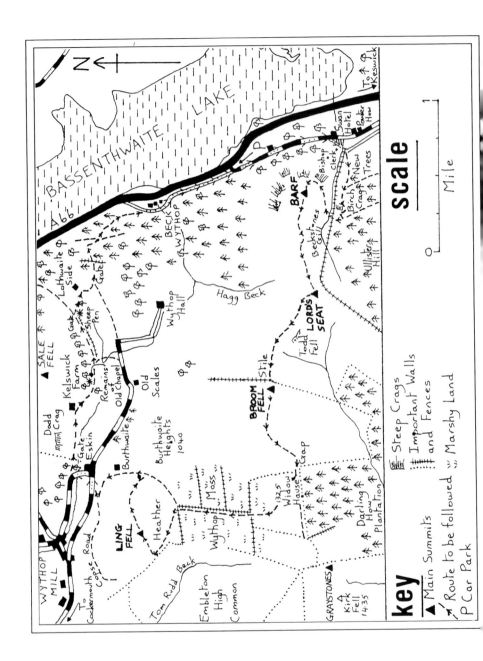

key

Main Summits ▲

Route to be followed ↗

P Car Park

⌇⌇⌇ Steep Crags

⊢⊢⊢ Important Walls and Fences

∵∵∵ Marshy Land

scale

0 ————————— 1 Mile

13. AROUND WYTHOP VALLEY

Start and Finish: A car park and picnic site opposite Hursthole Point, three quarters of a mile north of the Swan Hotel where the old Thornthwaite road joins the A66.

Summits Visited:		
	Barf	-1536 feet
	Lord's Seat	-1811 feet
	Broom Fell	-1670 feet
	Ling Fell	-1224 feet

Total Height Climbed: 2250 feet

Distance Walked: 10 miles

Nearest Centre: Thornthwaite

Map Required: Ordnance Survey English Lakes 1:25000, North West area sheet.

INTRODUCTION

Hidden from casual view to the west of Bassenthwaite Lake, the Wythop Valley remains a secluded backwater. This charming picture of forgotten Lakeland provides the ideal setting for a walk. Accessible at one point only via a narrow lane through the tiny settlement of Wythop Mill, the valley is largely unknown outside the immediate area. Its attraction for the solitary fellwalker is, therefore, obvious. Take time out to make the acquaintance of this idyllic, unspoilt locality and wander the rolling, grass-clad uplands with solitary confidence.

When approaching from Keswick, the viridity of the coniferous curtain is drawn apart to reveal the rough-hewn, craggy outcrop of Barf. This imposing edifice should in no way deter those who have placed unwavering trust in their intrepid guide. Your faith is well justified. The precipitous acclivity is easily avoided by taking advantage of the path to the left which accompanies Beckstone Gill to its source. Once the initial steepness up the western flank is achieved, all is easy going from then on.

It is perhaps worth noting that the serried ranks of conifers have conquered all the lower slopes hereabouts to the south and west. Their attempts to take over the upper fells and Wythop Valley have so far been resisted. It is hoped that this situation can be maintained for the future enjoyment of those such as myself who revere open fell country.

ROUTE DESCRIPTION

Make your way south for almost a mile down the old road to the Swan Hotel. A right-hand side road gives access to the path which ascends the unremitting slope through Beckstones plantation, the lower extremities of which compose a new planting of larch trees.

In plain view rests the elevated throne of the immortal Bishop of Barf surveying his diocese in company with the diminutive Clerk. Legend has it that a bet was made in the bar of the Swan to climb Barf on horseback. The inebriated punter only reached as far as where the Bishop now resides before a grand tumble down to the Clerk's domain. The resulting markers are preserved as eminent reminders of man's folly in attempting to intimidate this noble fell.

Passing to the left of the northern outliner of Birch Crag, the path turns sharp left above to enter the confines of the old spruce plantation bearing right in this enclosed twilight world up to the forest road. Immediately after crossing this broad highway, a fence stile gives access to the open fell. A short descent to ford Beckstones Gill is followed by an easy climb heading north west up the opposite heathery slope. Rounding the east face of Barf overlooking the lake, it is then a simple stroll across the knobbly top to gain the summit.

The next objective, Lord's Seat and the highest point on the walk, can be seen to the west. No doubt in times past, the noble aristocrat reclined here in peace, surveying the expanse of his domain. The path heads due west bearing left around the upper reaches of Beckstones then west south west across the broad grassy plateau to mount the east side of the Seat.

From the summit, descend the pathless tract heading north west to join a thin path circling the eliptical ridge above Tod Fell Crags to make a gradual rise onto Broom Fell.   A majestic, well-constructed beacon adorns an otherwise undistinguished summit and is gained after crossing the boundary fence by a stile.

The ridge continues round to the south west.   Follow a thin trail down across a shallow depression thence down a grass slope of increasing acclivity to the corner of Darling How plantation. Pass through a wide gap in the wall and make a pathless oblique descent of the bank heading north west below Widow Hause.   Head for the commencement of the central routeway which crosses the swampy morass of Wythop Moss, one of the most extensive of its kind in Lakeland and deserving of a far greater degree of infamy than is indeed the case.

A central causeway provides the only reasonable means of gaining the opposite bank without undue immersion of one's footwear.   After safely reaching the north side, take a handy sheep trod rising left through the heather to join the wall which crosses Ling Fell.   At the crest, a simple walk to the north east gives access to the stone trig column, floating in a sea of heather.

After a short easterly descent, a track is joined which leads down to the corpse-road contouring the base of the fell.   Turn left through a gate to gain the valley road beyond Burthwaite.   Turn right here then left at Eskin to reach the north side of the valley.   Another right becomes the farm road under the shadow of Sale Fell to Kelswick.   The path branches right to the south of the farm buildings, passing the ruined church in Chapel Woods.   A quarter mile beyond the woods, our way lies right to pass through a gate abutting a sheep pen, then past Lothwaite Side bearing left to enter Wythop Woods through a gate.

The bridleway continues east down into the dense forest, bearing right to join a major forest trail for a short distance before forking left down to Beck Wythop.   A simple stroll along the old road brings us back to the car park and the culmination of a delightful walk following an interesting route of ever-changing scenic beauty.

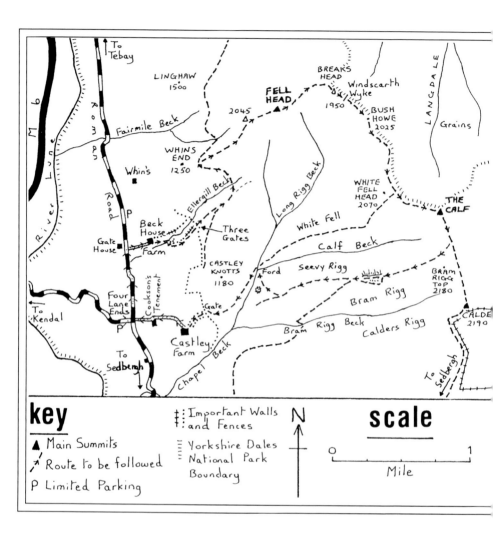

key

▲ Main Summits

↗ Route to be followed

P Limited Parking

‡ : Important Walls and Fences

≡ Yorkshire Dales National Park Boundary

N

scale

0 ——————— 1

Mile

14. THE CALF OF HOWGILL

Start and Finish: A roadside pull-in on the left, 50 yards down the western arm of Four Lane Ends, a junction along the old Sedbergh/Tebay Roman road.

Summits Visited: Fell Head   -2070 feet
                          The Calf   -2220 feet

Total Height Climbed: 1800 feet

Distance Walked: 7.5 miles

Nearest Centre: Sedbergh

Map Required: Ordnance Survey Pathfinder Series 1:25000, Sedbergh and Baugh Fell, Sheet No. SD 69/79.

INTRODUCTION

Having spent most of my hiking career in the company of the Lakeland fells, I have until recently become somewhat blinkered in my attitude to other fell walking country. Consequently, it was some time before I began to cast a curious eye towards that compact group of hills to the east known as the Howgill Fells. Lying outside the boundary of the Lake District National Park has precluded their inclusion in the itinerary of most visitors to the region. What a sad oversight it would be for anybody failing to acquaint themselves with these tranquil and relatively unfrequented fells.

The Howgills have an introverted personality which is an attraction in its own right. The silky smooth appearance and extensive grassy nature more akin to the moorland undulations of the Pennines, lacks the excitement and thrill normally expected from mountain environments. This, of course, is their inherent magnetism for those fellwanderers who, like myself, yearn for the solitude of remote places.

Lacking walls above the in-take fields, as well as distinguishing landmark features, one should think very carefully before attempting the ascent in heavy mist - an observation to make with the benefit of hindsight. A recent visit was almost abandoned when an already faint path over Breaks Head disappeared along with my map in the heavy rain. I have since carried a polythene cover on all my walks to prevent this happening again. Having retreated back over Fell Head in disgrace, a spectral figure in the form of a local solicitor appeared out of the murky gloom. His company and valuable guidance in locating The Calf were much appreciated on this occasion. Even with the help of a reliable compass, it is far from easy to maintain a correct course when all is grass amidst a rolling terrain.

ROUTE DESCRIPTION

From Four Lane Ends, head north along the old Roman road for a half mile before turning right towards Beckhouse Farm. One of the few public rights-of-way into the hills starts here - and three cheers, not a signpost to be seen. The path goes to the right of the farmhouse, crosses Ellergill Beck and heads sharp right out of the stream trough to follow a walled groove up to the in-take wall. Three gates provide access to the open fell.

The grass track keeps to the right of the beck before circling the valley head in a wide, left-hand loop climbing gradually round to Whins End Col. The main path continues on towards Linghaw, but our way lies up the west ridge on a distinct path, a steady uphill pull onto the subsidiary summit of Fell Head. Continue ahead to the main summit which has a much more distinguished cairn complete with its own flagpole.

All is grass around this solid edifice, but linger awhile to take in the dramatic western prospect towards Lakeland. The path over Breaks Head soon fades. The way lies south west descending to the pronounced gap of Windscarth Wyke. Here the path is picked up with the sharp pull over the bald dome of Bush Howe and is followed by an easy stroll across White Fell

Head up onto The Calf. The broad, plateau-like summit, complete with white trig column, has little to recommend it other than being the highest point of the whole range and the natural mecca for those who wander the Howgill Fells.

The main path continues south towards Calders, but at the depression bear right around the western edge of Bram Rigg Top to follow the long sweeping west ridge down over Bram Rigg. Descending Seevy Rigg, what has so far been an excellent path strangely fades away. Keep right, down the steepening grass slope to the confluence of Calf and Long Rigg Becks. Cross the stream to join the fell track coming off White Fell. This makes a slight ascent of no more than 200 feet around the southern slopes of Castley Knotts to reach the lowland pastures through a gate. The track enters a rough walled lane passing to the right of Castley Farm. Continue west down the made-up farm access road past Cookson's Tenement back to Four Lane Ends. Go straight across back to the car.

Although these fells are a joy to walk in clear weather, the ever present danger of losing one's way in bad conditions must never be overlooked. It is also imperative that this totally unspoilt landscape is maintained in its present state for future generations to enjoy.

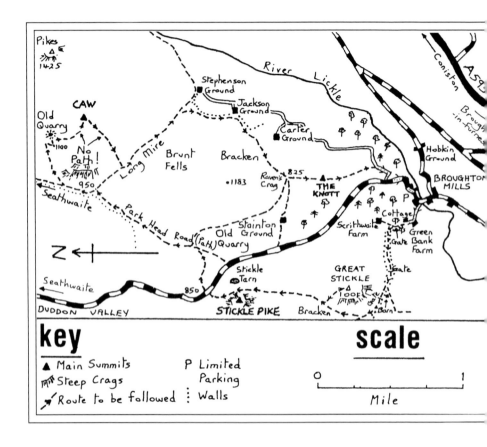

Pikes
△ ⌐
1425

CAW
△

Old Quarry
↑1100
No Path!
950

Seathwaite

Z ←

Seathwaite

DUDDON VALLEY

Long Mire

Park Head Road (Path)

850

Brunt Fells

Bracken

•1183

Stephenson Ground

Jackson Ground

Carter Ground

River Lickle

Raven's Crag

825

THE KNOTT
△

Stainton Old Ground Quarry

Stickle Tarn

STICKLE PIKE
△

GREAT STICKLE
△
1 OOF

Bracken

Barn

Scrithwaite Farm

Cottage

Grate Bank Farm

gate

Hobkin Ground

BROUGHTON MILLS

P

Coniston

A59

Brought -in-Furnes

key

- △ Main Summits
- ⋔ Steep Crags
- ↗ Route to be followed
- P Limited Parking
- ⋮ Walls

scale

0 _____ 1

Mile

15. THE DUNNERDALE FELLS

Start and Finish: Broughton Mills, a hamlet lying two and a half miles north of Broughton-in-Furness on the River Lune.

Summits Visited:		
	Stickle Pike	-1231 feet
	Caw	-1735 feet
	The Knott	-925 feet

Total Height Climbed: 2200 feet

Distance Walked: 7.5 miles

Nearest Centre: Broughton-in-Furness

Map Required: Ordnance Survey English Lakes 1:25000, South West area sheet.

INTRODUCTION

Lying between the Rivers Duddon and Lickle, in the south west corner of the Lake District, these fells are well off the beaten track and a considerable detour away from the main centres of activity is required. Their modest altitude means that they have a tendency to be overawed by their loftier neighbours and are consequently rarely visited by those who place height above quality.

Such an omission does a great disservice to this Lilliputian landscape, the rugged nature of which will be revealed by a study of the Ordnance Survey map. Outcrops occur in profusion, though none so great as to attract the hard rock climbers. The Dunnerdale Fells are by no means insignificant mole hills and possess all the essential ingredients that go to make up the best that is Lakeland - steep crenellated flanks fronting a distinctive pyramidal summit.

From across Morecambe Bay, the two main summits of Stickle Pike and Caw are easily identified. On a clear day, their conical forms, etched stark against an azure backdrop, are in no way intimidated by the elder statesmen holding centre stage.

On some of the sections of this walk, paths are sketchy and even lacking all together, a recommendation in itself if sufficient care is taken. Many of the well-established paths crossing the area were made by a past generation of indigenous fellsmen and are still mainly utilised by today's farming communities. Walkers are rarely encountered. The connoisseur who enjoys a challenge - and delights in his own company - will revel in the circuitous nature of this route.

ROUTE DESCRIPTION

Parking space for a few cars is available over the River Lickle in Broughton Mills where the road widens on the left. Take the narrow metalled road which leads past Green Bank Farm to a small cottage. Here the path enters a wood following the wall round through a gate - one of many hereabouts - onto the fell side. The way lies straight ahead up the facing slope for a short distance before turning left into a grassy, walled lane. Avoid the path forking right which heads for Scrithwaite Farm.

After passing through two more gates, the path forks at an old barn. Bear right up to yet another gate and follow the wall round the lower southern slopes of Great Stickle and on to the open fell at last.

The way now lies through dense bracken (if you arrive in summer) which is guaranteed to soak your trousers after a downpour. Note the bifurcation from the main track to Ulpha, which forks right up verdant slopes onto the undulating ridge. To the south east lies the prominence of Great Stickle crowned with a trig column and involving a return detour of less than a half mile over easy terrain.

Where the path fades, keep in a northerly direction. It will soon be picked up more distinctly as the compelling and assertive cone of Stickle Pike is approached. Rounding the upper reaches of the side valley occupied by Hare Hall Beck, the path climbs to a shallow depression on the east side of Stickle Pike. A frontal assault is discouraged by the brooding defiance of the south buttress which acts as a more than adequate guardian for this distinguished peak. Where the path begins its declevity, watch for the well worn ascent heading left up the final rise.

The summit is also easily gained from the fell road, the eroded path testifying to its popularity. That is cheating, however, and fails miserably to give full justice to this proud miniature mountain of character. The highest of the Dunnerdale Fells and the next objective can be seen across a bubbling sea of confused grey outcroppings one and half miles to the north east. Caw dominates the immediate vicinity, its magnetic configuration demanding attention from all who actively seek out the best of Lakeland's wild and lonely outposts.

After returning to the depression, continue in a north easterly direction to reach the fell road. Crossing the road, proceed through the old quarry grounds to join Park Head Road. This well graded old highway continues down to Seathwaite. Once a major thoroughfare, it has now been superseded by the present motor road but still remains an excellent route for hikers.

As the track descends to the Duddon Valley on the west flank of Caw, an obvious path forks right up to a disused slate quarry. The abandoned buildings and spoil heaps conjure up memories of a by-gone age when life was tough but rather more leisurely than that 'enjoyed' by Technocratic Man. When the narrow fell path above the workings fades, continue straight up the steep slope of Caw. Another trig column perches on the highest point indicating the obvious importance given to these fells by the Ordnance Survey as viewpoints. Indeed, when conditions are right, the roof of England is vividly portrayed against the northern skyline and beckons invitingly, stimulating one's appetite for a future expedition.

There are no paths off the summit. Make your way in a south westerly direction down into Long Mire to join the valley path. This branches right before a cross vale wall is reached, over to the west side of the valley passing Jackson and Carter Grounds. These family farmsteads enclosed the common pastures belonging to the monks of Furness Abbey and are unique to this area.   They are consequently among the oldest agricultural settlements to survive from medieval times.

The path climbs gradually through the bracken to a small col continuing round the base of Raven's Crag.   A thin path heads due south to cross The Knott before descending sharply to the farm road.   There follows a short road walk back to Broughton Mills and the culmination of a day to be remembered for its peace and tranquillity.   Enjoy and savour this opportunity to wander over unspoilt territory, remote from the established tourist trails.

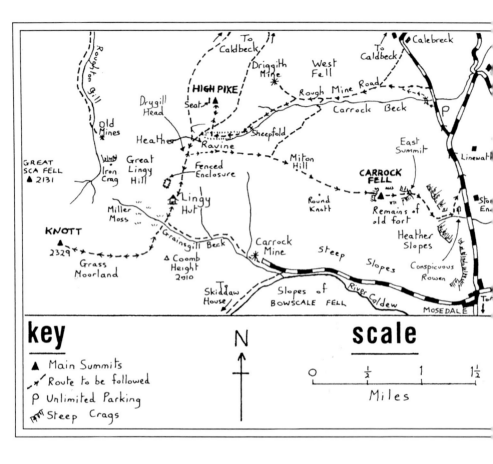

key

- ▲ Main Summits
- ✦ Route to be followed
- P Unlimited Parking
- ⋔ Steep Crags

N

scale

0 — ½ — 1 — 1½

Miles

16. THE CALDBECK FELLS

Start and Finish: The fell road betwen Mosedale and Caldbeck is unfenced with ample parking space on the grass verges.

Summits Visited:

High Pike	-2157 feet
Knott	-2329 feet
Carrock Fell	-2174 feet

Total Height Climbed: 2450 feet

Distance Walked: 11 miles

Nearest Centre: Hesket Newmarket

Map Required: Ordnance Survey Landranger Series 1:50000, Penrith, Keswick and Ambleside areas, Sheet No. 90.

INTRODUCTION

The commanding presence of Skiddaw and Blencathra belie a group of fells in the north which display a gentle reticence distinctly out of character with their extrovert cousins. Separated from the main fell country of Lakeland by the Vales of Bassenthwaite and Keswick, these uplands form an isolated mass of independent form and personality all their own. Once the glossy facade is stripped away, one may be forgiven if a lack of enthusiasm is not immediately forthcoming. But much of interest lies hidden amidst the grass and heather-clad moorlands, and needs to be teased out of these reluctant stalwarts.

Those who demand the dramatic sculpturing associated with the frost shattered pinnacles of Lakeland's core, will indeed be disappointed if they mistakenly venture into this austere landscape.

Usually referred to as the fells ' back 'o Skidda', these northern rolling uplands are largely pathless and unfrequented. Do not under estimate this extensive bleak wilderness, however. The way is often long and arduous with few landmarks to act as a guide if bad weather unexpectedly drops in (as it frequently does in Lakeland), keeping us on our toes and dispelling a complacent attitude.

Only when the walk was completed did I realise that not a single wall or fence had barred my way. Although the industry of early dry-stone wallers is to be marvelled at, and the artistry of their creation admired, the obstructive nature of these barriers is an anathema to those who relish the open freedom inherent in fell country. However, I must admit that in bad weather conditions, their guiding hand is more than welcome to distraught travellers who have lost their way.

ROUTE DESCRIPTION

Not even the fell road is walled so park anywhere between Stone Ends and Carrock Beck. Crossing the stream by a small footbridge, work your way through the bracken to join the old road leading to the disused mine workings at the head of the valley. The track heads due west on the north side of Carrock Beck.

At the valley head, a path crosses the beck following the right hand bank of a tributary that emerges from a ravine high on the left. Proceed up the lip of the high stream banking, moving down into its bed immediately past a sheepfold. Do not be surprised to have an escort of wary sheep keeping pace on the edge of the ravine. Like a patrol of Red Indians in a western movie, they obviously suspect the motives of these strangers intruding on their territory. On the occasion I passed this way, there was little evidence of the stream that had caused this abrupt gully in an otherwise moorland environment.

At the head of this unusual yet fascinating fissure, exit right and head due north up a gentle grass slope onto the no less interesting crown of High Pike. Here, one may tarry awhile, resting on a seat dedicated to the memory of a local fell lover, Mick Lewis. It is more likely, however, that the nearby stone shelter will be preferred in view of the wind-swept nature of these fells. Other features of interest include a stone trig column and the ruins of an old shepherd's cottage. The extensive panorama allowed the summit to be granted the status of an official signal beacon in the days when communications were rather more primitive, but no less eye-catching, than in modern times.

Heading due south, join the well worn track that traverses the east flank of High Pike through bilberry and heather down to Lingy Hut. Once an old shooting hut, it now acts as a welcome refuge for weary travellers. Complete with its own visitors book for all to sign, it provides a detailed history of movement across these fells in recent years. Don't forget to lock the door when you leave.

Now is the time to decide if the long trudge onto Knott is worth the extra time and effort involved. Only you can decide. Peak baggers will not hesitate, and I must confess that on this occasion my boots were guided by this latter motive. On a circular walk akin to all those in this volume where the start and finish is one and the same, long detours of this type are a rarity and not recommended as a matter of course. The commanding height and centrality of Knott, rather than any aesthetic quality, acted as a magnetic force that I for one found irresistible, even with the summit dome under a leaden shroud of mist.

If you are assailed with similar vibes, then descend to the swampy crossing of Grainsgill Beck. A thin path climbs the steep bank above Miller Moss bearing west along the broad shoulder. It disappears among the extensive grass tussocks which are hard going even though the gradient is minimal.

From the summit cairn of Knott, it is necessary to retrace one's footsteps back past the hut and over Great Lingy Hill as far as the ridge known locally as Drygill Head. Leave the main track and head east to join another path that swings round the upper reaches of the ravine. This path, though rather wet underfoot in parts, is quite straightforward visiting the stony oasis of Miton Hill en route to the craggy ramparts of Carrock Fell - a delectable eminence with its very own ancient hill fortifications and a firm personal favourite.

A continuous mound of stones with four gaps which appear to be gateways into this prehistoric citadel rings the summit area. The presence of its past residents can almost be felt in periods of quiet meditation in the late afternoon sunshine. After returning these astral images to the appropriate resting place in one's subconscious, cross to the east summit which lies beyond the boundaries of the fort.

Descending the steep east face on a thin track, one cannot fail to be moved by the brilliant splashes of purple daubed on this heather-clad canvas in full bloom.   The artistic talent of nature displays this final curtain call to perfection in late summer.

A dry, grass gully provides the key to the final phase. After 250 feet of descent, look out for a lone rowan tree atop a small crag on the left.   A charming path leaves the confines of the gully just above this conspicuous landmark and slants down across the stony east face to the road.   A brief stroll back to the car ends a walk infused with all manner of delicacies to tempt the walker's palate.

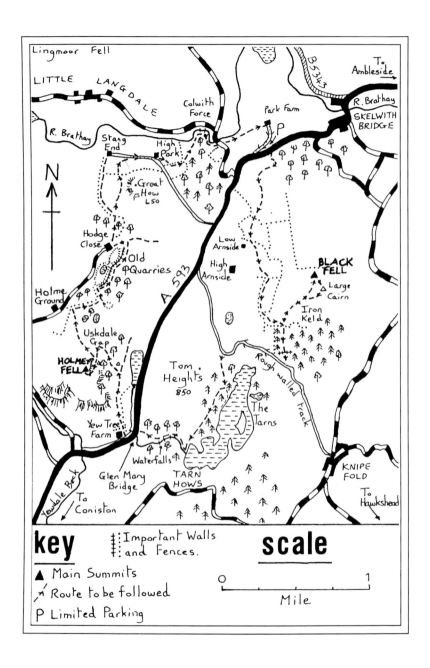

17. FELL SANDWICH

Start and Finish: A roadside pull-in on the right of the A593, one mile west of Skelwith Bridge on the way to Coniston.

Summits Visited:	Black Crag	-1056 feet
	Holme Fell	-1040 feet

Total Height Climbed: 1500 feet

Distance Walked: 9 miles

Nearest Centre: Elterwater

Map Required: Ordnance Survey English Lakes 1:25000, South East area sheet.

INTRODUCTION

In the normal course of events, one would expect the more remote fell walks to be located on the periphery of the region. Yet even close to the heartland, it is still possible to wander at will over unspoilt fell country without the ever-present fear of unwelcome intrusion into one's meditations. Black Crag and Holme Fell have all the attributes that are to be found on fells accorded the distinguished honour of mountain status.

Sandwiched between the major centres of Ambleside and Coniston, they offer walking country of the highest quality in miniature. For those who on this occasion do not feel able, or willing, to tackle the big boys in the vicinity, this pair of lightweights provide sport to silence the most biased of critics.

It is pleasing to note that these lesser fells (in altitude only) are frequently overlooked in the mad scramble for height.

As for Tarn Hows, what is there to say that has not already been said a thousand times. A place that all solitary fell walkers should visit once in their lifetime, its over exposure will certainly rekindle one's appreciation of the lonely outposts in Lakeland. This famous beauty spot was, for me, a disappointing filling in an otherwise scrumptious sandwich.

ROUTE DESCRIPTION

Walk back up the A593 towards Skelwith Bridge for 150 yards - no pavement so beware - then take the path on the right signposted to Borwick Ground. Bearing up to the right then left in a southerly direction, the path climbs gradually for a half mile to a wall. Go through the gate bearing right up the facing grass slope to meet another wall coming up from the right and joined by a path ascending from the Hodge Close access road.

Passing through the wall gap close to Low Arnside, the path then veers away across open ground heading south east to meet another wall. After this gap, follow this wall south accompanying it round towards Iron Keld with the plantation on your right. Before this distinctive knoll where the path enters the confines of the plantation, bear left to follow a splendid path across the hummocky summit plateau heading north. The trig column mounted on an airy rock pedestal is gained after a short climb up the final rampart.

This route to Black Crag follows the easiest course across the western flank of the fell, approaching the apex from behind. Three generations of Dugdales recently completed this section with no catastrophes other than a broken thermos flask - the work of the youngest member of the family. Here is a perfect opportunity for septagenarians and beyond to notch up at least one Lakeland fell summit. Take your time and enjoy the expansive panorama that reproduction in books can never hope to capture.

Return to Iron Keld via the large cairn which is plainly in view to the south. Then bear right to rejoin the summit path and savour a well deserved action replay. Continue due south over the fence stile into the confines of Iron Keld plantation. The haunting nature of enclosed conifers adds an eerie quality to the walk down to the rough road which crosses this southern side of the fell. Obviously once an important routeway, it gives some idea of the communication difficulties of past generations. After gaining the road over another fence stile, turn right and follow it down for a half mile as far as the Tarn Hows path on the left immediately beyond a stream on a sharp bend.

Three hundred yards along this path, one enters the woods on the west side of The Tarns over a fence stile. As the tarn shore is approached, take the distinct trail branching right away from the water's edge making its way through the woods heading south west. After joining the shore the track widens and continues up to the car park. At the footbridge over the debouching waters of The Tarns, we head right, alongside crashing cascades, on a path that provides ample compensation on the descent to Glen Mary Bridge.

Crossing the main road from the car park, walk towards Coniston for two hundred yards before taking the path on the right by the side of Yew Tree Farm. Holme Fell presents a solid indomitable front, but the daunting prospect of its conquest should in no way act as a deterrent. After crossing a stile, head north leaving the Skelwith path at a large, unmistakable cairn to slant left up a charming route through the trees bearing round to the west. Uskdale Gap is approached via a broad gully and then we are on the plateau. Bear left through the heather towards the craggy ramparts above taking a south south westerly direction passing well to the right of the dominating cairn on Ivy Crag. A short scramble up the rocky east face gives access to the summit ridge.

The rugged panorama of mountain Lakeland is laid out in style to the north. Such views serve merely to strengthen my profound good fortune for having been granted the privilege of residence in this unique corner of England. To vacate the ridge, head north for a short distance bearing right down a broken crag to rejoin the upward path at the foot of the east face. Alternatively, retrace your steps then bear north west to take an easy stroll down towards Holme Ground arriving at a wall which skirts the western base of the fell.

Go right to follow this wall round through woodland to Hodge Close Quarries. Pass to the east of the two yawning chasms which are the result of an insatiable demand for slate that has now virtually ceased as a major commercial enterprise in favour of tourism. A solid fence acts as an effective deterrent preventing the over curious from suffering an untimely demise in the murky depths. A gate gives access to the rough road left to Hodge Close itself. Here turn right and head north into a small wood. This final section of the walk from Hodge Close is outlined in detail on the enlarged map opposite.

After passing through the gate at the far side of the wood, the main track bears left alongside a wall. Our way lies straight ahead across a grassy common to the left of a wide swamp - the elevated prominence of Great How dominating the immediate horizon beyond the swamp to the east. After crossing a fence stile, descend to a metalled road, turning right along it towards High Park Farm. Branch left here across a cattle grid then through the fields and three gates taking advantage of the wooded path which passes the plunging waterfall of Colwith Force. After joining the Elterwater road, turn right for 50 yards to take the path heading left across a field bound for Skelwith Bridge. The path crosses a stile and climbs a steep, wooded bank above the River Brathay. After another stile, the path crosses an open field gaining a metalled access road through a further stile which returns us to the A593. Turn left back to the car.

Take advantage of the total experience that this 'fell sandwich' has to offer. The constantly changing vista at every corner provides a tasty repast not to be missed.

To Little Langdale

Colwith Force

Path climbs steep wooded bank

River Brathay

Stang End

High Park

Signpost to Hodge Close

Double Stile

Signpost to Skelwith Bridge

A593

To Ambleside

To Coniston

Little Fell

Great How

The Dubs

Abandoned Farm Machinery

Hodge Close

Key

S Stiles

G Gates

φ Prominent Oak Tree

△ Prominent Cairn

P Roadside Pull-in

Woods

Bracken

Marsh

N

0 ½

Mile

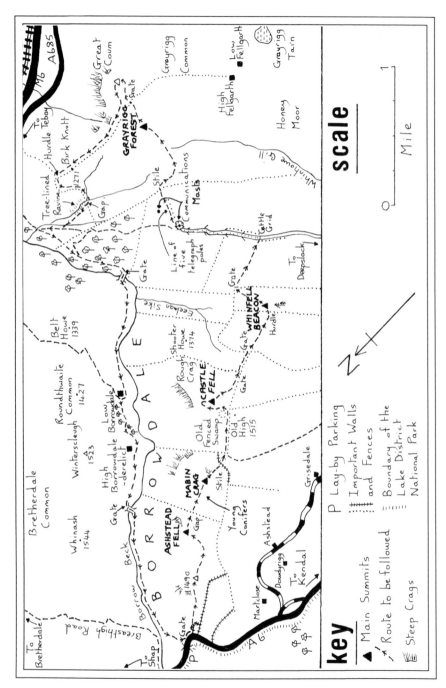

key

▲ Main Summits

‑‑‑ Route to be followed

🌲 Steep Crags

P Lay-by Parking

⪤⪤ Important Walls and Fences

⋯⋯ Boundary of the Lake District National Park

scale

0 _____ 1

Mile

18. THE WHINFELL RIDGE

Start and Finish: A lay-by complete with telephone box on the left of the A6 before Huck Bridge where the road bisects the Borrowdale Valley.

Summits Visited:		
	Ashstead Fell	-1530 feet
	Mabbin Crag	-1580 feet
	Castle Fell	-1560 feet
	Whinfell Beacon	-1544 feet
	Grayrigg Forest	-1620 feet

Total Height Climbed:	1630 feet	
	With Grayrigg	
	Forest	-1930 feet

Distance Walked:	8.5 miles	
	With Grayrigg	
	Forest	-12.5 miles

| **Nearest Centre:** | Kendal |

Map Required: Ordnance Survey English Lakes 1:25000, South East area sheet.

INTRODUCTION

Sandwiched between the major highways of the A6 and M6, the five sisters of Whinfell present an unpretentious image to the citizens of Kendal. These shy, retiring maidens possess a hidden depth of charm found only by those who seek to avoid the flirtatious reputations of their more extrovert cousins to the west.

Upon closer acquaintance, one can quite easily understand the reluctance that has been forthcoming with regard to the courtship of these fair damsels. But that, of course, is their inherent attraction for gentlemen such as I who prefer the absence of rival suitors.

The other main attraction concerns the domain over which these reticent ladies preside. Borrowdale continues to be one of the most natural valleys in Cumbria with its classic, glacier-carved form remaining thankfully unscarred by the ravages of twentieth century man. The absence of a motor road into the valley must be considered a major asset in this respect. The farm track to Low Borrowdale - the only inhabited settlement in the valley - provides walkers with an excellent return amidst the passive inactivity of a landscape suspended in the mists of time.

All those who wander the remote outposts of rural England should be grateful to the concerned bodies who fight to retain our past heritage in its natural state. It is to be hoped that the suggestion to drown Lower Borrowdale has now been consigned to an appropriate dustbin reserved for such incogitant proposals.

ROUTE DESCRIPTION

Walk back from the lay-by to where the road crests the ridge. Passing through a gate on the left, make your way up the steepening incline alongside a fence on your right. This is soon left behind as the strengthening path climbs up this steepest section of the walk towards the south east on to the subsidiary summit of Ashstead Fell. This superior cairn should not, unfortunately, be mistaken for the main summit which lies a half mile to the south east along a thin eliptical path rounding Comb Hollow.

From here Mabbin Crag can be seen across the depression - the crag in question overlooking Borrowdale and hidden from view. The way to Mabbin Crag continues south east through a gap in the broken cross ridge wall and up the grassy slope between rows of newly planted conifers to the neat cairn surmounting the summit.

Dropping down to the next depression amidst more conifers, cross a fence stile and make for the corner of a wall on the right of the ridge. One wonders what will become of this section of the walk over Mabbin Crag in years to come as the baby trees grow towards maturity. It is to be hoped that this commercial enterprise makes some provision for the walking fraternity. Pass through a gap and proceed alongside the wall as far as an old fenced swamp. A detour onto the aptly named Castle Fell passes between its dual turrets and is best approached from the rear.

A south facing grass causeway returns us to the wall. Keep left of the wall until the second of two gates lying a quarter mile apart. An easy stroll up the facing open slope gives access to the rocky top of Whinfell Beacon. A fenced gap in the summit wall gives immediate access to the senior matron in the group with her twin badges of authority. A thin path heads due east down to a gate by a wall corner and continues across the undulating moorland towards the communications mast. Unfortunately, a cross wall bars direct progress.

Even where a considerable deviation from the direct route is necessary to achieve the next objective, clambering over obstructions that are lacking gates, stiles or gaps to assist movement across private farm land cannot be condoned, even when they lie across rough upper pastures. Boundaries are often erected for the containment of animals and farmers incur a considerable amount of needless trouble and expense when such means of enclosure are destroyed. Please stick to the recognised route, therefore, to help maintain the country code and ease the way for future generations who hope to make use of these walks.

Having digested this entreaty, take the distinct track that heads south east to the tarmac road necessitating a descent of 300 feet. Turn left up this road to the Telecom station. Conservation groups have sadly been unsuccessful in their efforts to prevent a smaller yet no less obtrusive structure being erected a quarter of a mile to the east. We could well do without this battle of the air waves on our hallowed fells. One wonders why this area was not included when the original boundaries of the National Park were formulated. Perhaps some knowledgeable reader could provide enlightenment.

The decision must now be made as to whether one has the inclination or stamina to continue. Prudent individuals who wish to make a strategic withdrawl should follow the bridleway down into Borrowdale.

A series of telegraph poles behind the Telecom mast points the way to a cross fell wall. After traversing the wall stile, work your way to the right in a wide curved sweep round the head of the small tributary valley and up the pathless incline to join the tallest sister on Grayrigg Forest. Having come this far, it would be remiss of you not to visit the large monument a half mile to the east commanding a superb prospect over the Lune Gorge towards the Howgills. The path descends to a north/south wall crossing the summit plateau and is negotiated via a small gate. Meandering out of the shallow depression around a series of small knolls, the noble edifice is soon reached.

Return to the wall working your way around the craggy upper reaches of Little Coum and follow the wall down the north ridge over Birk Knott keeping to the right side. At its T-junction, a gap gives access along another wall bearing left into a side valley. After crossing the stream through the wall gap, the path heads down towards the farm road on the left of a ravine. Bear left away from this when the path fades joining a clear track which slants down to the right after fording a narrow rivulet.

Turn left along the main access road (rough) to Low Borrowdale Farm on the left of Borrow Beck. After three quarters of a mile, the track crosses to the right bank over a substantial bridge. The bridleway enters the farm yard and exits through a gate at the rear into a narrow copse where it is joined by another major right-of-way from Roundthwaite. Continue past the abandoned farm of High Borrowdale on your right to recross the beck via another bridge a half mile beyond.

Approaching the main road, the track bears left away from the beck to climb out of the valley, gaining the A6 through a gate. On this final haul back to the car, savour the captivating atmosphere of this unspoilt landscape, its quality of timeless appeal helping to ease tired limbs on the return journey.

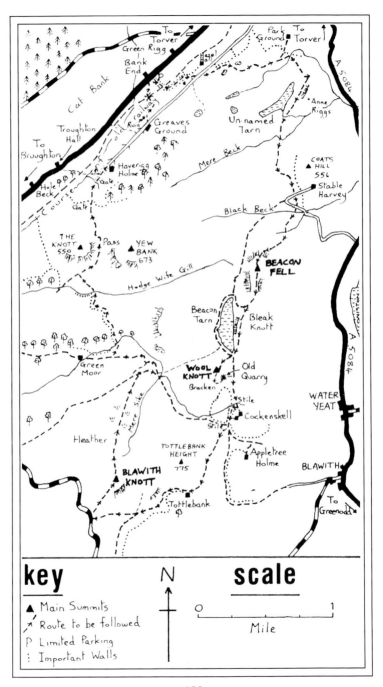

key

▲ Main Summits
↗ Route to be followed
P Limited Parking
⋮ Important Walls

N

scale

0 ——————————————— 1
Mile

19. THE BLAWITH FELLS

Start and Finish: A roadside pull-in adjacent to the rough lane on the left of the A593 at Bank End, one and a half miles south west of Torver.

Summits Visited:	Beacon Fell	-836 feet
	Wool Knott	-730 feet
	Blawith Fell	-806 feet

Total Height Climbed: 1500 feet

Distance Walked: 10.5 miles

Nearest Centre: Coniston

Maps Required: Ordnance Survey English Lakes 1:25000, South West area sheet **and** Ordnance Survey Pathfinder Series 1:25000, Broughton-in-Furness and Newby Bridge, Sheet No. SD 28/38.

INTRODUCTION

Approaching Torver from the south, one cannot fail to be impressed by the classic proportions outlined against the rugged skyline ahead. The Old Man of Coniston has attracted visitors for countless generations, and the day you arrive will doubtless be no exception.

Those of us who relish our own company should turn aside at Torver and take note of the fells to the south. An extensive triangle of rough ground, it demands attention with its efforts to drive a wedge between the Crake Valley and Torver High Common. At first glance, the Blawith Fells appear as a poor substitute for the brash guardian of Coniston. But this deceptive landscape conceals its true character, reserving the experience for those who make the effort to become more closely acquainted.

Although of only modest height, this trio of knobbly peaks refuse to be overawed by their loftier more showy neighbour to the north. Thrusting out of the lonely moorland, their assertive presence cannot fail to inspire the care-worn traveller. The only place that other walkers are likely to be encountered is around the delectable expanse of Beacon Tarn - a liquid jewel nestling between the points in the crown and understandably popular.

The difficulties involved in any expedition do not necessarily stem from the ruggedness or altitude of the terrain. The walk herein described covers a wide variety of scenery and requires concentration at all times if the correct route is to be maintained. The level of difficulty emanates from the meandering nature of the many paths that need to be followed amidst an undulating landscape that can confuse the mind with its innumerable outcrops of similar appearance. Unlike the high fells where the objective is rarely in doubt, a circuit of the foothills produces its own problems which require an equal measure of care and attention.

ROUTE DESCRIPTION

Pull off the road just before Bank End and park on the left by the grass lane which crosses the old railway track. Over the track, the path bears left through a gate and up an easy slope towards Hazel Hall with the wall on your left. Here a tarmac road is crossed at an angle, the track heading across open moorland in an easterly direction between a cluster of diminutive tarns.

When a large un-named tarn comes into view just before the northern boundary in-take wall, the path along its eastern bank is joined. Although a constituent part of Torver Low Common, this tranquil stretch is no common pond and is deserving of an aristocratic title - any suggestions? Head south towards the distinctive cone of Beacon Fell. Rounding the western slope of Tottle Bank, the hairpin bend on the metalled access road to Stable Harvey is crossed and recrossed.

Once over Black Beck, a good path progresses upward through an interesting rock gully onto the summit clothed in a confusion of heather and grass. Descending the south ridge, delightful Beacon Tarn appears quite suddenly. Bear right down to the northern edge of the Tarn, then proceed along its west bank to climb up onto Wool Knott - a peaceful, rarely visited summit to take one's ease, where time stands still and one's watch becomes a redundant appendage.

A thin path heads south from the summit but is difficult to follow as it bears left through heavy bracken. A small disused quarry is soon reached and thereafter follow an easy descent to the ford near Cocken Skell. Those of modest height who do not relish the possibility of disappearing in the bracken jungle, should return to the tarn and take the main path due south.

Through a gate, the path turns sharp right away from Cocken Skell, along a walled lane, then across a field to a wall stile. From here, the main path heads south east accompanied by a wall towards Blawith. Our route bears right up a bracken-covered slope to contour around Tottlebank Height, joining a rough fell road at the farm of the same name. Note that this Tottlebank is all one word unlike the Tottle Bank previously encountered. Head west along this track around the base of Blawith Knott until a distinct grass path is reached branching from the main track which heads south, the in-take wall on its left. This path leads directly to the fell road from where a well-used path points the way to the top of Blawith Knott.

From the summit cairn a thin path heads north across an open wilderness of heather devoid of all human presence - definitely not the place to break a leg. Turn left at the valley depression to follow the main bridleway down Mere Sike. Take a right branch before Green Moor to follow the southern in-take wall around to cross Hodge Wife Gill. The path heads north west leaving the meandering wall and adjoins a major fell track over the unusual pass between The Knott and Yew Bank. A gentle descent brings us to another in-take wall. Keep this on your right to gain the metalled farm road beginning at Haverigg Holme.

Leave the road at a ruined barn on the left opposite Greaves Ground to take a track through the fields passing under the disused railway back to Bank End. This completes an expedition of character and merit which should test your map reading abilities - and the clarity of my description.

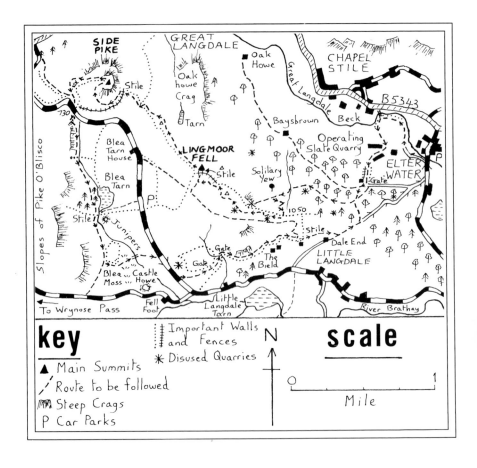

key

▲ Main Summits

╱ Route to be followed

⛰ Steep Crags

P Car Parks

⋮ Important Walls and Fences

✳ Disused Quarries

N

scale

0 ——————— 1

Mile

Map labels:

SIDE PIKE

GREAT LANGDALE

CHAPEL STILE

Oak Howe

B5343

Stile

730

Oak howe Crag

Tarn

Baysbrown

Great Langdale Beck

Operating Slate Quarry

ELTER WATER

P

Slopes of Pike O'Blisco

Blea Tarn House

LINGMOOR FELL

Stile

Solitary Yew

Gate

Blea Tarn

P

1050

Stile

Junipers

Gate

Stile

Dale End

LITTLE LANGDALE

Stile

Gate

The Bield

Blea Moss

Castle Howe

To Wrynose Pass

Fell Foot

Little Langdale Tarn

River Brathay

20. LINGMOOR FELL

Start and Finish: An official free car park in the village of Elterwater.

Summits Visited:

	Lingmoor Fell	-1530 feet
	Side Pike	-1187 feet

Total Height Climbed: 1900 feet

Distance Walked: 8 miles

Nearest Centre: Elterwater

Map Required: Ordnance Survey English Lakes 1:25000, South West area sheet.

INTRODUCTION

A parabolic mass of distinctive green slate, the craggy bulk of Lingmoor lies sandwiched between the dual valleys of Langdale. Greater Langdale must remain the most popular of Lakeland valleys, being the mecca for all manner of visitors throughout the year. The smaller yet no less imposing twin of Little Langdale conceals a multiplicity of charms hidden from casual view. This diminutive dale has never attracted an extensive retinue and continues to be overshadowed by its big brother to the north. This, of course, is a first class reason for introducing this unspoilt valley to the discerning walker.

The Lingmoor ridge provides a picture-postcard view of the most famous panoramic skyline in the District. Instantly recognisable from any direction, the Langdale Pikes display their extrovert proportions to an admiring public. Side Pike affords a perfect station to observe the exquisite sculpturing of these mighty heights chiselled to perfection by the elements of time.

ROUTE DESCRIPTION

After crossing Great Langdale Beck, turn right down the quarry access road. Take a well made path alongside the wooded stream on the left of a wall which bears left round to the working slate quarry yard. Pass by the buildings taking note of the industrial activities in operation - a rare sight indeed as the vast majority of quarries have been abandoned. Quarrying, although an activity that is indigenous to the region, is a conflict of interest along with tourism, water supply and forestry that requires tight control in order to comply with the conservation aims of the National Park.

After coming to terms with this industrial heartland of the Langdale Valley, head south for the rough forest road leading to Baysbrown. After a short distance (about thirty yards) down this road, a path can be seen rising left through the woods. This soon joins an old quarry trail which heads right, to the open fell and continues up to the extensive spoil heap on the skyline.

Immediately opposite an obvious evergreen tree, take a path on the left that meanders up the fell to a wall accompanying the north rim of this elongated ridge. Turn right over the stile and follow the edge up onto the crest past further abandoned quarry workings. The knobbly summit of Lingmoor Fell is gained immediately after crossing a fence stile.

The distinct path continues down the steeper and infinitely more rugged north west ridge alongside a wall. Ahead, Side Pike beckons invitingly. At this point, attaining the summit appears a short and easy, if craggy, scramble - an illusion that is soon dispelled as this rock-girt turret is approached. Like the mythological sirens, this deceptive temptress will also lure the unsuspecting traveller to an untimely end. In order to gain the apex of the tower, a considerable descent and re-ascent is necessary, amply rewarded by the splendid views. First cross the fence stile and follow it down until a right fork which allows us to ascend the gently graded west shoulder onto the summit.

A wall leads unerringly down to the fell road which connects the two Langdale valleys. Cross straight over and follow an easy path through the wooded grove adjacent to Blea Tarn. With the Pikes forming a perfect

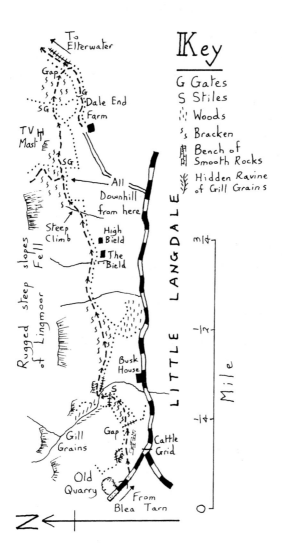

To
Elterwater

Gap

G
Dale End
Farm

SG

TV
Mast

SG

All
Downhill
from here

Steep
Climb

High
Bield

The
Bield

Rugged steep slopes of Lingmoor Fell

Busk
House

S

Gill
Grains

Gap

Cattle
Grid

Old
Quarry

From
Blea Tarn

LITTLE LANGDALE

Key

G Gates
S Stiles
Woods
Bracken
Bench of Smooth Rocks
Hidden Ravine of Gill Grains

m|₂
Mile
-|₂
-|₄
0

N

107

backdrop, this vision of scenic enchantment is included in virtually all the pictorial guides to Lakeland. And like all well known beauty spots, it is best visited at off-peak times.

After crossing the wall stile at the southern boundary of Blea Tarn Woods, accompany the west bank of Blea Tarn Beck past a prominent crag on the left. The path now bears left, away from the beck on its way to join the Wrynose Pass road. Upon meeting a wall coming up from the beck, we accompany it leaving the main path where this wall forks left down to a sheepfold forming a corner point. Cross Blea Moss and the beck making use of a handy footbridge 150 yards east of the fold.

After rejoining the fell road, follow it down to the right for 300 yards past a disused small quarry on the left. Take the distinct farm track a little beyond the old quarry. This delightful yet rather switchback trail follows the outer edge of the in-take wall along the northern side of Little Langdale under the shadow of Lingmoor's steeply shelving south flank and is fully illustrated on the enlarged map section on the previous page.

The path descends to join an old fell road just beyond Dale End Farm. Take a left here to pass through Sawrey's Wood and down the rough walled lane, joining with the metalled access road to Baysbrown. Continue down a further 200 yards to the Elterwater road whence a left will return us to the village.

Although one cannot hope to remain in total seclusion on this walk, it does provide an opportunity to enjoy the tremendous profile of this justifiably renowned valley from a relatively unfrequented location. The vast majority of visitors tend to congregate on or around the environs of Great Langdale and the Pikes. Little Langdale continues to remain the preserve of the connoisseur.

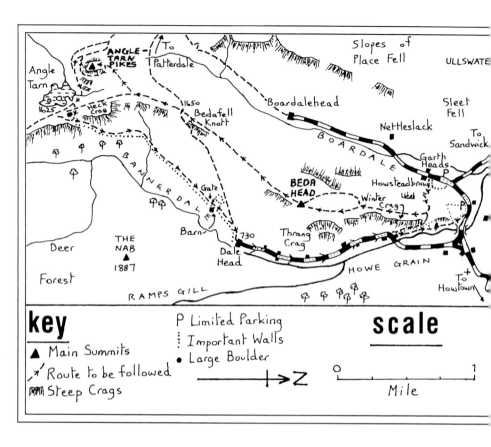

key

▲ Main Summits
↗ Route to be followed
⛰ Steep Crags

P Limited Parking
⋮ Important Walls
● Large Boulder

⟶ Z

scale

0 _____ 1
Mile

21. AROUND MARTINDALE

Start and Finish: A small pull-in on the left at the northern end of the Beda Fell ridge on the road connecting the valleys of Boardale and Howe Grain.

Summits Visited: Beda Head   -1664 feet
                        Angletarn Pikes   -1857 feet

Total Height Climbed: 1500 feet

Distance Walked: 8 miles

Nearest Centre: Pooley Bridge

Map Required: Ordnance Survey English Lakes, 1:25000, North East area sheet.

INTRODUCTION

It never ceases to amaze me how much faith we place in predictions made by those champions of the isobar, the weather men. With voices raised in ecstatic glee when clear skies are forecast, we set forth with a light heart and high hopes for some classic camera shots.   But how frequently such childlike anticipation is crushed beneath a suffocating mantle of mist and rain.

Such has been my fate on more occasions that I care to remember on my trips across the fells.   Prevailing westerlies are the main culprits.   The Lakeland walker does indeed require the patience of Job in his travels across the roof of England together with copious quantities of that vital ingredient - eternal optimism.   I make no excuses in my preference for fair weather hiking. The certainty of aesthetic stimulation and peace of mind is worth the unwelcome possibility of chance encounters with others of a similar mind. With most of the walks completed in this book, the odds have been thankfully in my favour. You may not be so lucky so be prepared for a close acquaintance with the grey stuff.

Martindale, one of those little known regions of the Lake District, remains hidden from general view. As well as lying off the main highway which runs beside Ullswater, the valley is protected by a gear-crunching hairpin system of no mean gradient. Its popularity is, therefore, reserved for those discerning walkers who had the good sense to purchase this auguste volume.

ROUTE DESCRIPTION

After a half mile walk down the Boardale road to Howsteadbrow Farm, a grass path between the lower walled enclosures gains access to the open fell via a stile and works its way up to the crest of the ridge. Turn south here to follow a thin yet interesting track (is there any other so long as it leads somewhere?) along the upper edge of Winter Crag. Beda Fell presents its most impressive face to the east which drops steeply into the valley of Howe Grain.

The path divides beyond Winter Crag after a period of level walking and either way can be taken. Both lead up to the lumpy, uninteresting summit of Beda Head which does not quite live up to the excellent approach. The gently graded path continues in a south westerly direction along the wide ridge and is easily followed in mist.

Immediately after negotiating the knobbly uplift of Bedafell Knott the main bridleway to Patterdale is crossed. If your visit was under the same austere conditions as mine and you are feeling less than satisfied with the day's outing, turn left to follow the track down to the road end at Dale Head.

Those who retain the true spirit of persistent expectation in the hope that things can only improve should continue south to meet the popular High Street route on the east side of Angle Tarn. In clear conditions, bear right as the ridge culminates in its highest point across the hummocky terrain to reach the loftiest of the twin Pikes which have adopted the name of the tarn. The first of these impressive rocky prominences is the higher and is easily negotiated up the slanting north slope. It is then but a short if steep descent to the main path around Angle Tarn.

When visibility is minimal, it is left to individual discretion as to whether finding this illusive peak is worth the ever-present danger of losing one's way. If you decide to persist turn right by a large boulder where the ridge path terminates at the tarn along the well worn track towards Patterdale. It will soon bear round to the west for a quarter mile before heading due south. After 100 yards, leave the track to go right up the grass slope - compass bearing, north east. At this point a thin path should be located tending left between the twin Pikes and bringing you to the abrupt rock face of the main summit. A reversal of the directions should return you to the prominent boulder on the east side of the tarn. This is certainly not the simplest of manoeuvres.

Pride having been assuaged, or discretionary excuses made, take the thin path heading due east. A wall is soon located which points the way down into the remote yet hauntingly beautiful upper reaches of Bannerdale. The path accompanies the wall under Heck Crag and down to the lonely farm-house at Dale Head where the old cross-fell trail to Patterdale begins.

The road walk down Howe Grain is enlivened by savouring the quiet isolation of this superb valley sculpted in the traditional mould of the Lake District. The natural beauty of the landscape is also safeguarded by a scarcity of garish footpath signs. Those that do exist are discretely placed and made from local slate.

At Winter Crag Farm, take the path bearing left away from the road to follow the western side of the valley accompanied by a wall on the right all the way to the Boardale/Howe Grain link road. A short stroll to the left will return you to the car.

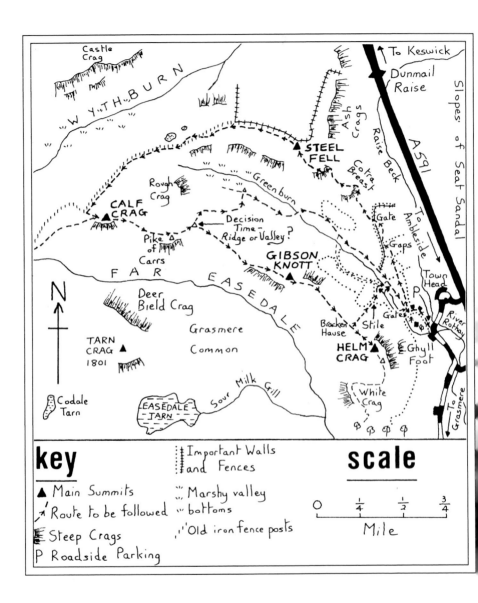

key

▲ Main Summits

🖌 Route to be followed

🖌 Steep Crags

P Roadside Parking

┆┆ Important Walls and Fences

🖌 Marshy valley bottoms

🖌 Old iron fence posts

scale

0 — ¼ — ½ — ¾

Mile

22. AROUND GREENBURN

Start and Finish: Limited parking is available at the hamlet of Ghyll Foot where the access track to a pair of cottages and the Greenburn Valley begins.

Summits Visited:		
	Steel Fell	-1811 feet
	Calf Crag	-1762 feet
	Gibson Knott?	-1379 feet
	Helm Crag?	-1299 feet

Total Height Climbed:	1830 feet	
	With Gibson Knott	
	and Helm Crag	-2250 feet

Distance Walked: 6 miles

Nearest Centre: Grasmere

Maps Required: Ordnance Survey English Lakes 1:25000, North East and South East area sheets.

INTRODUCTION

Grasmere remains one of the most popular villages within the National Park. Yet barely two miles to the north, the shy, retiring valley of Greenburn lies hidden from view, being rarely visited and therefore an ideal objective for the discerning few. Only through close investigation can the serenity be fully appreciated.

Approaching from the south, the visual impact of Helm Crag with its battlemented summit captures the eye - and the imagination. This deceptive little scorpion should be handled with care and discretion, however. Being the only Lakeland fell that involves a rock climb to capture its summit provides a sting in the tail which cannot be ignored.

The highest of the tops to be visited on this circuit is Steel Fell which controls the Pass of Dunmail. Legend has it that Dunmail, a Saxon King of Cumbria, fell in defence of his realm at this strategic location and a pile of stones marks the exact spot where his remains are supposed to be buried.

Even in this renowned core of the region, it is still possible to avoid the crowds and escape into beautiful if not so remote countryside. A brief encounter with the unfrequented environs in and around Greenburn will calm the most tremulous of constitutions. Who could possibly imagine that the busiest highway through the central Lakes lies no more than a single mile from this hallowed and secluded location.

ROUTE DESCRIPTION

Access to the enchanting Greenburn Valley is gained from the rough land which passes to the right of a wooded enclave. Immediately past the two old cottages - one of which has the distinction of being Elizabethan - a gate unlocks the mysteries of this unspoilt fantasia.

Turning right, the path makes its way via a series of gaps through the disintegrating lower in-take wall up the south east ridge of Steel Fell. The open fell lies through a kissing gate stile in a strong boundary fence. Ahead, the knobbly backbone of Dunmail's vigilent sentinel remains to be scaled. The ribbed vertebrae stretch upward in a series of rock steps culminating in a confusion of stony outcropings atop the undulating summit.

A fence following the old Cumberland and Westmorland county line passes across the highest point. The path heads west accompanying the fence around the north rim of Greenburn. When the fence turns down into the Wythburn Valley, continue ahead along the line of ancient iron posts past a scattering of marshy tarns.

Leave these helpful guides at a distinct cornering of the fence to head left onto the obvious summit of Calf Crag. The rugged south flank cannot be fully appreciated on this approach.

The gnarled and twisted clenched fist of Helm Crag can be seen punching the clouds two miles distant at the far end of this superb ridge. Continuing due east, the ridge narrows and improves as progress is made. Upon reaching the cairned depression beyond Pike of Carrs, a decision must be made. For those who have never previously made the pilgrimage to Helm Crag, the continuance along the ridge to this famous bastion is recommended. Returning to Bracken Hause, the steep but easy descent into the lower reaches of Greenburn poses no problems.

Having passed this way before on numerous occasions, I now invariably elect to bear left at the depression and follow the line of small cairns down a well graded pleasant path into Greenburn Bottom. In this enclosed monastic world, those worries about the pay rise that never came hardly seem to matter. The nectar of pure ozone imbibed in open country is guaranteed to clear the most befuddled of brains.

Head south east down the valley before crossing the beck near a ruined sheepfold. The path moves away from the stream bearing right to continue in a more distinct manner back to the in-take walls. A short walk down the rough access lane returns us to Ghyll Foot - and back to the real world.

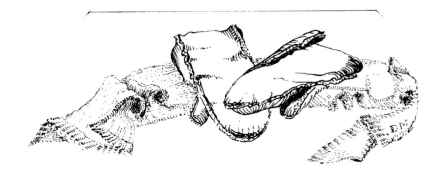

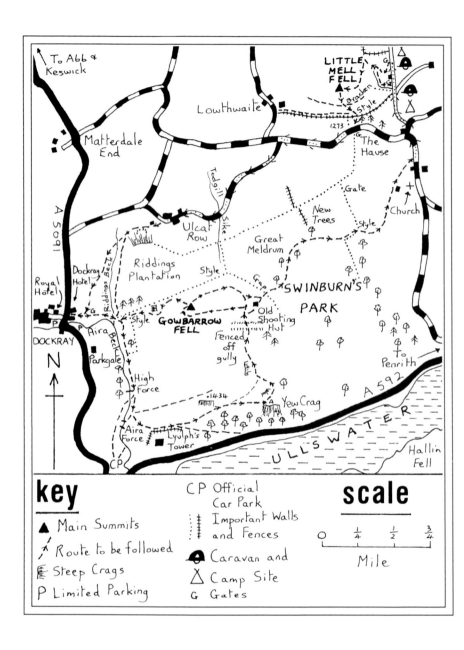

To Abb &
Keswick

LITTLE
MELL
FELL

Lowthwaite

Bracken
Stile

1273

Matterdale
End

The
Hause

Gate

A 5091

New
Trees

Church

Tadgill Sike

Ulcat
Row

Great
Meldrum

Style

Riddings
Plantation

SWINBURN'S

Royal
Hotel

Dockray Beck

Dockray
Hotel

Style

PARK

Riddings Beck

G

Style

GOWBARROW
FELL

Old
Shooting
Hut

DOCKRAY

N

Aira Beck

Parkgate

Fenced
off
gully

To
Penrith

High
Force

A 592

14.34

Yew Crag

Aira
Force

Lyulph's
Tower

ULLSWATER

CP

Hallin
Fell

key

▲ Main Summits

✗ Route to be followed

Ɛ Steep Crags

P Limited Parking

CP Official
Car Park

⋮ Important Walls
and Fences

⌂ Caravan and

△ Camp Site

G Gates

scale

0   ¼   ½   ¾

Mile

118

23. SWINBURN'S PARK

Start and Finish: The hamlet of Dockray which lies one and a half miles north of Ullswater along the A5091.

Summits Visited: Gowbarrow Fell   -1579 feet
                        Little Mell Fell   -1657 feet

Total Height Climbed: 1750 feet

Distance Walked: 10 miles

Nearest Centre: Glenridding

Map Required: Ordnance Survey English Lakes 1:25000, North East area sheet.

INTRODUCTION

The delights to be enjoyed on this walk do not rest with the attainment of the highest points but with the unusual line of approach. One of the most charming footpaths in Lakeland wends its merry way around the steep, rugged flanks of Gowbarrow Fell towards Little Mell Fell. Possessing all the qualities to be expected in a Rolls Royce of fell paths, every step is a joy to be savoured at one's leisure. Take your time to fully appreciate its firm underlying foundation, narrow meanderings through delectable scenery and ever changing landscape overlooking the classic valley of Ullswater, and well graded progression throughout.

The Meldrum section of the path provides a unique link between the two fells that lie across this open wooded tract. Each can be regarded as a separate walk in its own right if this is to be preferred or can be combined in the more extended route described in this chapter.

The summit of Little Mell Fell is rather an anti-climax - an ocean of grass mounted in a bracken frame. It remains an isolated outlier on the north western edge of the National Park along with its slightly loftier twin, Great Mell Fell. Neither of these stranded whales is likely to attract attention from anyone other than reclusive hermits and readers of this book - if there is any difference. Little Mell provides an excellent objective as part of this unfrequented circuit above Ullswater, and also as a self-contained short climb when time is of the essence.

The rolling environment of Gowbarrow is also a let down after sampling the tasty starter. Having the tourist playground of Aira Force as a major attraction on the west side has caused the lower slopes to become a favourite sojourn of picnicers. The heathery plateau, however, receives few visitors and the summit itself has a certain aesthetic charm of its own being the appetizer to be lingered over prior to the main course.

ROUTE DESCRIPTION

Limited parking is available on the road verge opposite the Royal Hotel in the charming old world hamlet of Dockray, and also on the right adjacent to Aira Beck opposite the track to Watermillock Common immediately south of the bridge. The path to be taken lies between the Dockray Hotel and an old farm which offers a choice of beverage at the end of a satisfying day on the fells. But first the walk.

Go down the rough walled lane past Millses. Follow the path around the bend of Aira Beck crossing Riddings Beck via a footbridge and proceeding towards the celebrated waterfalls. They are indeed spectacular and it is left to individual choice as to whether a visit is undertaken. Below High Force, the path passes through a wooded area before bearing east along the fenced boundary of woodland which fronts Low Force.

As the crenellated ramparts of Lyulph's Tower come into view, bear left to ascend the side of Gowbarrow Fell. The main path continues ahead to visit the hidden precipice of Yew Crag - a favourite haunt of budding rock climbers - and down to the main road. The initial steepness is soon over and the path gives ample opportunity to admire the eastern prospect over Ullswater. Before heading north, a visit is recommended to the prominent cairn crowning the top of Yew Crag which plunges into the sylvan mattress below.

Towards the end of this eastern flank of Gowbarrow, an unusual fenced off section has to be negotiated. The path has been swept away at this point by flood water pouring down this acclivitous gully - the awesome power of nature asserting her normally dormant presence and reminding us of the forces constantly at work in shaping this unique landscape.

Descend towards the ruins of the old shooting hut then turn left and head due west up the grass path which leads to the summit of Gowbarrow Fell. If this is as far as your aspirations go, then move north west through the heather to join the cross fell wall and accompany it down to the valley. The path avoids Airy Crag, bearing left around this abrupt obstacle. A stile at a wall corner adjoining a small plantation returns you to the Aira Force path and thence back to Dockray by the same outward route.

Little Mell beckons hopefully across the Park to the north east inviting exploration by a quiet minority who will not disturb its pastoral charm. Leave the summit on the wall side of the fell which bears right returning to the shooting hut. Passing through a gap in the wall, the path contours around the eliptical open wooded slopes arriving at a cross wall. Keep alongside this on its left for 100 yards whence a stile allows the continuation of the through route to the fell road.

Turn left for 200 yards, then right at Cove Cottage on the opposite side from the caravan site. Another left leads past a further caravan/camping site. Take a left fork after 200 yards to hopefully arrive at the fence surrounding Little Mell Fell, the ascent of which is nowhere near as daunting as it appears on this approach.

Pass through the gate at the left of the junction south of Folly Cottage and follow the right bank of a stream which bears right joining a cart-track above the cottage. As an alternative route for those who might prefer to take advantage of well established tracks, continue ahead past the old quarry as far as a gate set back on the left where the metalled road ends. A deeply rutted tractor track heads back south west for 100 yards before bearing sharply right aiming for the corner of a fence which ascends the fell side from the access road.

When the fence corner is neared, turn south and take a thin path slanting obliquely up through the bracken. In its upper stages, the path bends right to a sheep repose where the bracken gives way to rough grazing. The stone trig column lies to the west across the gentle verdant swell. Although a featureless grassy wilderness, this is a place of rare solitude to be prized for its sense of peace and the opportunity for airy meditation. After asserting one's conviction that the best things in life are indeed free, head due south down an increasingly acclivitious grass bank to join a distinct path contouring this south side of the fell. A further path forks right heading down a bracken corridor over a fence stile to reach the road pass called The Hause.

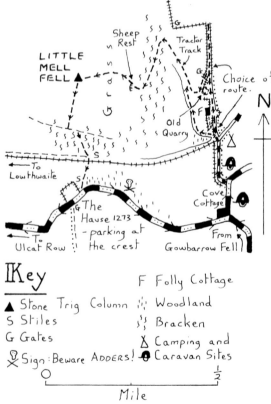

Key

▲ Stone Trig Column
S Stiles
G Gates
⚡ Sign: Beware ADDERS!

F Folly Cottage
⠿ Woodland
⁏⁏ Bracken
Δ Camping and
⊕ Caravan Sites

O ————————————— ½

Mile

Ample roadside parking is available on the south side of The Hause from whence the circuit around Little Mell Fell can be commenced by walking east down the road to Cove Cottage. Make use of the enlarged map on the opposite page for this section of the walk. Take note that the trees on the left contain an abundance of Britain's only poisonous snake, the adder, whose bite carries a high risk health warning.

If you are returning to Dockray, descend west from the pass for a half mile, turning left down the lane to Ulcat Row. Immediately past the church in this tiny hamlet, take the track on the left which makes its way below the abrupt crags on the northern flank of Riddings Plantation. Another enlarged map below provides detailed directions for this rather confusing section through the in-take fields back to base. If time is on your side, perhaps some liquid refreshment at one of the Dockray hostelries will complete the perfect end to the perfect day.

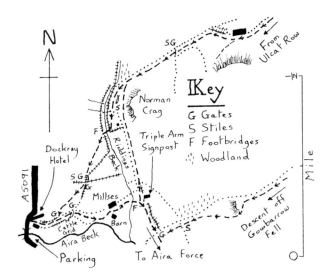

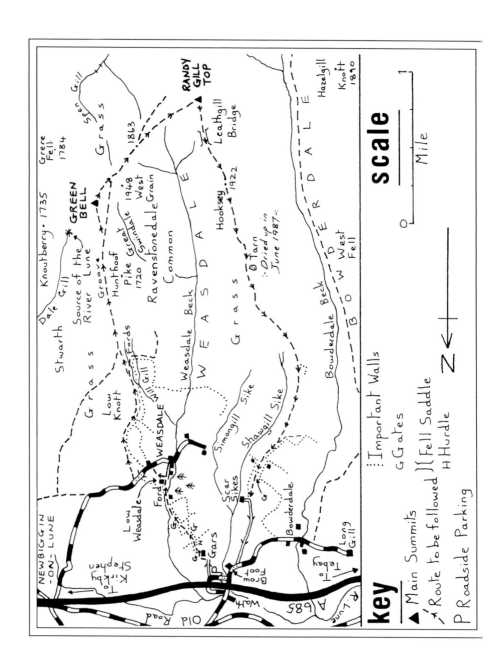

key

▲ Main Summits

⌁ Route to be followed

P Roadside Parking

∶ Important Walls

G Gates

)(Fell Saddle

H Hurdle

scale

0 _____ 1

Mile

N

24. WEASDALE HORSESHOE

Start and Finish: Adequate parking is available on the roadside immediately after turning right off the A685 for Bowderdale.

Summits Visited:	Green Bell	-1985 feet
	Randygill Top	-2047 feet

Total Height Climbed: 1530 feet

Distance Walked: 8.5 miles

Nearest Centre: Newbiggin-on-Lune

Map Required: Ordnance Survey Pathfinder Series 1:25000, Tebay and Kirkby Stephen, Sheet No. NY 60/70.

INTRODUCTION

The Howgill Fells still remain a safe refuge for solitary walkers. These northern valleys, to the east of Tebay in particular, together with their separating ridges, offer easy walking across a gentle swell of verdant pasture much frequented by sheep and fell ponies. Rocks are a prized phenomena amidst the waves of moorland grass, and crags assume the illusive quality of a fabled El Dorado.

Once a route through the low level maze of in-take fields has been negotiated, the upper slopes are an open range with unrestricted access. The horseshoe walk herein described provides an excellent circuit around the deep valley cut by Weasdale Beck and its associated tributaries. Advantage is taken of the parallel ridge tracks used by farmers to reach the higher rough grazing pastures around this unfrequented dale head.

A total lack of identifiable landmarks across this moorland wilderness renders it distinctly unsuitable for misty conditions. The chances of a circular ramble become an undeniable impossibility. There is no joy to be gained from such blind wanderings. Therefore, reserve it for a day when the pastime of identifying distant Lakeland sentinels whilst reclining atop the gentle giant of Randygill can be pursued at one's leisure.

ROUTE DESCRIPTION

Take the narrow farm road to Gars, turning left into the farmyard. A gate gives access to the bridleway which is now little more than an overgrown depression, and barely used even by modern walkers. The locked gates and disintegrating hurdle (all easily negotiated) give one the distinct impression that the local landowner has forgotten about this route being a public right of way.

After accompanying the lower reaches of Weasdale Beck for a short distance, the path makes a rather annoying decision to ford the stream. Obviously intended as a crossing point for farm vehicles, humble walkers who do not wish to risk testing the water-resistant properties of their boots at such an early stage should take advantage of handy, mid-stream boulders about thirty yards upstream.

Having gained the east bank, hopefully with dry feet, continue south towards Low Weasdale. Immediately after leaving the confines of this sylvan estate, turn left off the metalled access road along a rough track which soon joins the main road linking the remote hamlet of Weasdale to the A685. Turn left along this highway for 300 yards until a track heading south on to the open fell is reached. If you have got this far without going astray, a pat on the back is in order for excellent map navigation ability using the enlarged map section of this initial phase on the opposite page.

This track bears right following a wall into the minor valley of Will Gill. Before the wall and track cross to the other side of the valley, leave its

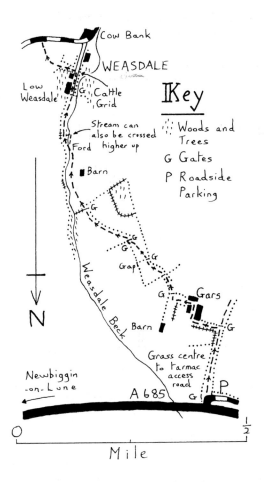

comforting presence and make your way across pathless grass slopes to join
another fell track 200 yards to the south east. This grassy rake continues
uninterrupted, if a little indistinct at times, to the head of Weasdale Valley.
The ascent is a gradual climb becoming more grooved on the east side of
Hunthoof Pike. The track then heads across to the other side of the ridge
contouring around Green Bell to avoid the summit. It is but a brief detour
to take in this unpretentious mound that has at least been granted the
distinction of a white trig column. The surrounding ring of stones makes
it an awkward back rest, thus discouraging any thoughts of langour.

127

A good path heads south west from the summit to rejoin the main track which passes behind the intervening shoulder of West Grain. Where the path bears left away from the direct ascent onto Randygill Top, continue ahead up the main east ridge. At last - a mountain topping the magic 2000 feet with a real cairn to repose against. On the day I arrived, the numerous sheep were most put out at having to vacate their elevated domain. Once alone, the silence was as complete as I have ever known it - not a breath of wind or murmer of distant traffic to disturb this idyllic moment.

Heading due north, the descent to Leathgill Bridge assumes the characteristics of a roller coaster. The abrupt declevity, on a narrow path, levels out at the saddle to rise again up the opposite bank onto the crest of the elongated ridge of Hooksey where a fell track begins. Progress down this grassy sward is pacy. Watch for the indistinct section where the tractor marks bear left to sweep round in a wide arc following the west side of the shallow valley of Shawgill Sike.

Half a mile beyond an unusual, dual-sided section of walling, the track reaches the first in-take walls of the lowland pastures. Passing through a gate, the metalled road providing access to Scar Sikes is reached. A further half mile past Brow Foot Farm returns us to our starting point.

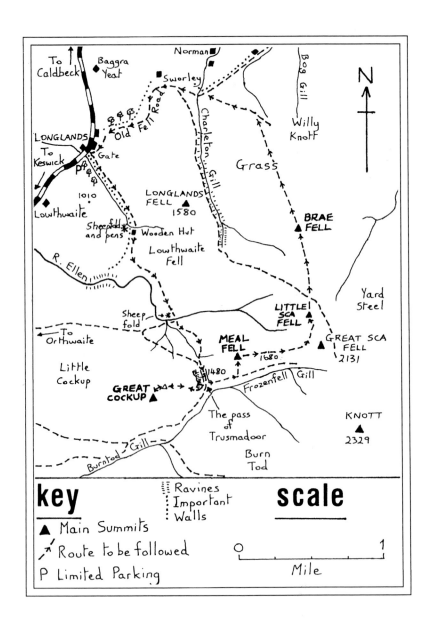

key

▲ Main Summits

↗ Route to be followed

P Limited Parking

⋮ Ravines
⋮ Important
⋮ Walls

scale

0 ————————— 1

Mile

25. THE ULDALE FELLS

Start and Finish: A right hand pull-in immediately before Longlands, near a small cluster of buildings on the road to Caldbeck.

Summits Visited:

Great Cockup	-1720 feet
Meal Fell	-1770 feet
Little Sca Fell	-2050 feet
Brae Fell	-1920 feet

Total Height Climbed: 1750 feet

Distance Walked: 7 miles

Nearest Centre: Uldale

Map Required: Ordnance Survey Landranger Series 1:50000, Penrith, Keswick and Ambleside areas, Sheet No. 90.

INTRODUCTION

On this walk, I promise not to mention the unpredictable nature of Lakeland weather, except to give myself a complementary pat on the back for some excellent navigation with map and compass. Although having the advantage of good lead-in paths, the upper reaches of the fells at the back of Skiddaw are rolling and grass clad. In consequence, one's compass becomes essential for locating mist-shrouded summits.

These fells lack the total excitement craved by those who frequent the more spectacular heights of the region. This, of course, is their saving grace. Silence reigns supreme amidst these remote fells which epitomise the true character of Lakeland, noisy highways and tourist trails having been left far behind.

An interesting anomaly that serves to stimulate one's enjoyment of the walk is the delightful pass of Trusmadoor. This craggy enclave, clearly seen on the approach from Longlands, cuts deeply into the surrounding green wilderness, a welcome show of strength in this gently shelving landscale.

The moderate gradients coupled with a high start make this a means of attaining the magic 2000 foot contour with relative ease.

ROUTE DESCRIPTION

After negotiating the stile close to the roadside pull-in, take the clear path which accompanies a wall to a cluster of sheep pens. Pass to the left of a small wooden hut - obviously for the use of busy shepherds and not lazy fellwalkers who have only just set off. The path soon leaves the wall for open country and contours round Lowthwaite Fell towards the tributary confluence of the River Ellen.

Cross the main stream near an old sheepfold, bearing left round a spur into a side valley. The narrow path climbs up the left side of the valley to Trusmadoor. Continue through the pass to avoid the rough scree slope. Then bear right taking a thin track through the heather which heads due west up the desolate slopes of Great Cockup before fading in the grass. From a lower cairn, the actual summit lies to the south west and is marked by a small mound of stones - an essential prerequisite for the top of any fell where the exact point would be in doubt.

Returning to Trusmadoor, remember to keep right of the direct line to Meal Fell in order to avoid precipitous crags flanking this side of the pass. Follow the rising track alongside but above the north bank of Frozenfell Gill for about a quarter mile before heading due north to gain the obvious summit of Meal Fell. This fine stony top is crowned by a circular rock shelter - a welcome refuge to consume one's picnic as the name suggests.

The next objective lies due east across a wide grassy depression and up the regular slopes of Great Sca Fell. Join a path that slants across this slope from right to left up to the shallow gap between Little and Great Sca Fells. A short walk to the north west brings one to the lesser but by no means overawed height of Little Sca Fell with its much more distinguished summit.

The easy stroll to Brae Fell first heads north crossing the old bridleway which once served as the access road to the large scale mining activity in the Caldbeck Fells. Bearing slightly west of north, the gentle swell of the broad ridge rises gradually to the distinctive cairn and should pose no problems in thick mist even though no path exists.

Once the stony oasis of Brae Fell summit is left behind, maintain the bearing of north north west on the long descent over extensive grass slopes which is quickly accomplished. Make use of a track slanting downhill from right to left joining the old fell road which has now been superseded by a metalled highway. Turn left along it for the return to Longlands, a mile distant.

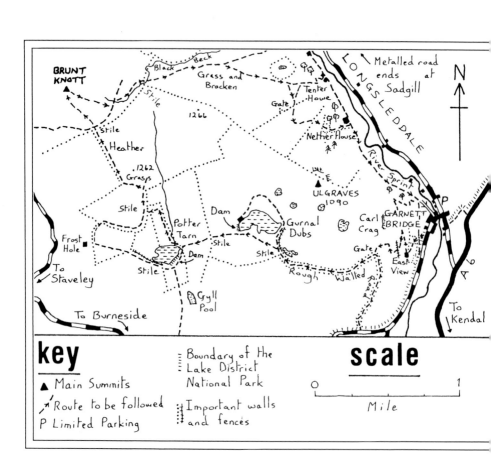

key

▲ Main Summits

✗ Route to be followed

P Limited Parking

⋮ Boundary of the Lake District National Park

⋮ Important walls and fences

scale

0 ————————— 1

Mile

26. STRICKLAND ROGER

Start and Finish: The delightful hamlet of Garnett Bridge which guards the narrow entrance to the valley of Longsleddale.

Summit Visited: Brunt Knott   -1400 feet

Total Height Climbed: 1100 feet

Distance Walked: 7.5 miles

Nearest Centre: Kendal

Map Required: Ordnance Survey English Lakes 1:25000, South East area sheet.

INTRODUCTION

The unpretentious, rather shy image displayed by the fell country to the north of Kendal has meant that this area is virtually unknown territory to those living beyond the immediate locality. Fellwalkers from afar ignore these timid hummocks in their quest for the nobility and spectacle of the region's rugged heartland but charms there are in profusion for those who take the trouble to delve beneath the surface. Tarns and extensive heather-clad uplands provide walking for the searcher after solitude. Wallow in the isolation of this lonely bastion of Lakeland by-passed by all save the solitary few.

As an ageing fellwalker well past his prime, I must confess to a preference for clear conditions - and an easy life. The days when I actively sought out potentially hazardous situations are long since gone. I make no apologies, therefore, for taking full advantage of walls and fences when the hills are shrouded in a dense mantle of cloud and welcome their friendly assistance on such occasions with open arms.

There is no pleasure in losing one's way in a featureless terrain such as that encompassed by the Strickland Roger plateau where faint paths mysteriously disappear in the swirling grey cloak. On one visit to this desolate arena, having foolishly forgotten my compass (even guidebook writers are human and fallible) it was more luck than good judgement that led me down the correct path into Longsleddale. So be warned - always go prepared for any eventuality.

ROUTE DESCRIPTION

A short way past the bridge at Garnett, a small pull-in on the right provides parking for two vehicles. Return to the road junction and take the Burneside road to the right for 150 yards to a signpost which points the direction across the pathless fields in a south westerly direction. The way slants uphill across the rising slope towards the abandoned farm buildings called East View. Take advantage of the enlarged section to guide you across this initial confusing terrain. This derelict settlement is well named on this flank of

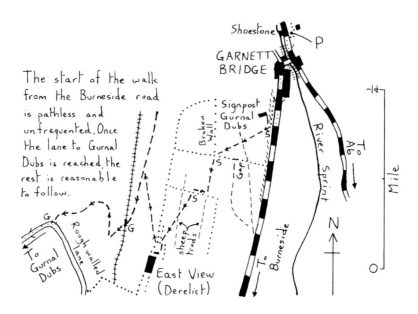

the plateau. The path then proceeds north west to join a more substantial track which meanders across the upper fields to meet the rough walled lane providing vehicular access to Gurnal Dubs - a rustic name for an attractive tarn.

At the end of the enclosed section of this lane, a gate leads to more open country, the hummocky verdure stretching away to the northern horizon. Bearing right, keep on this main track alongside a fence until a left fork indicates the way to Gurnal Dubs which is much used by local anglers. Passing the tarn dam, the path heads for a wall which tops the rising ground before its descent to Potter Tarn.

Keep to the northern edge of the tarn and follow the left side of a wall heading up the grass slopes on a fell track. At the top end of the field, go west to cross a hurdle and thence north again on the left of another wall to the open fell. Where this wall turns east, leave the main path to go north west over rough grass. Keep straight ahead when the path fades. Another path is joined at a wall corner which should be followed through the heather to a cross wall stile.

On my first visit to the area at this point, the mist decided that I had seen enough of this knobbly wilderness, but not before allowing me to note the position of Brunt Knott - north north west from the stile. Just as well, for once the Staveley track had been crossed, all was grassy and pathless. After experiencing the spectral tranquillity of total silence on the highest point, I returned to the main track down to Longsleddale.

Avoid a red herring going left. Instead, keep on bearing right to negotiate the wall alongside Black Beck. A sketchy path, becoming more distinct as height is lost, heads west through grass and bracken. There are few landmarks to take note of but resist any tendency to drift to the left until you have passed through the first wall gate. The path then bears left round a knoll through another wall gate and down a steepening gradient to Nether House Farm in the valley.

Turning right, follow the bridleway through the in-take fields back to Garnett Bridge. Make use of the enhanced detail on the larger scale map of this vague section shown on the following page.

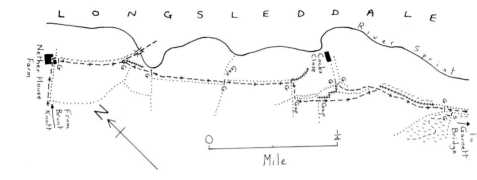

I have since revisited this special corner of peripheral Lakeland to more fully appreciate the natural, unspoilt nature of the landscape - in clear conditions of course - and will no doubt return again.

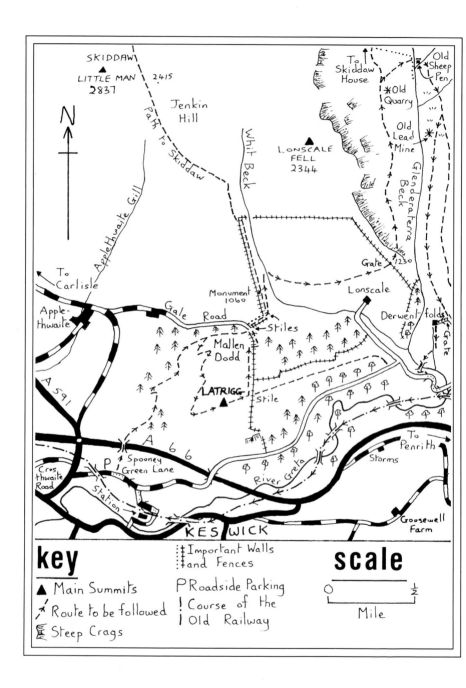

SKIDDAW
LITTLE MAN 2415
2837

N

Jenkin Hill

Path to Skiddaw

Applethwaite Gill

Whit Beck

LONSCALE FELL
2344

To Skiddaw House

Old Sheep Pen

Old Quarry

Old Lead Mine

Glenderaterra Beck

To Carlisle

Apple-thwaite

Gale Road

Monument 1060

Stiles

Gate 1230

Lonscale

Derwent-folds

Gate

A 591

Mallen Dodd

LATRIGG

Stile

To Penrith

A 6 6

Spooney Green Lane

River Greta

Storms

Cros-thwaite Road

P

Station

KESWICK

Goosewell Farm

key

▲ Main Summits

↗ Route to be followed

Steep Crags

Important Walls and Fences

P Roadside Parking

Course of the Old Railway

scale

0 ————————— ½

Mile

140

27. BEYOND LATRIGG

Start and Finish: Park in the first lane left after turning into Crosthwaite Road from the A66 roundabout to the north of Keswick.

Summit Visited: Latrigg   -1203 feet

Total Height Climbed: 1250 feet

Distance Walked: 9.5 miles

Nearest Centre: Keswick

Map Required: Ordnance Survey English Lakes 1:25000, North West area sheet.

INTRODUCTION

Motoring down the A6 from Penrith, a panoramic extravaganza opens up ahead with all the mountains in northern Lakeland jostling for pride of position. From Blencathra round to the Coledale Fells, the splintered horizon of jagged peaks is a magnetic attraction hard to resist. Very few people do, and consequently fail to take note of the lesser heights in this gargantuan world.

Approaching this spectacle, the discerning walker who relishes the isolation of his own company might well notice from afar the wide swathe scarring the east ridge of Grizedale Pike. Generations of booted pedestrians have worn this ever-widening highway and are likely to continue to do so. Such observations are a common occurrence on many of the high fells and may encourage kindred spirits to look aside for a more satisfying if less spectacular promenade.

Closely associated with the town of Keswick, and a local favourite, Latrigg is easily climbed by all from eight to eighty. As an appetizer to the circuit of the Glenderaterra Valley, Latrigg is unsurpassed. The simple yet satisfying walk into the middle reaches of this wild and lonely country separating Skiddaw Forest from Mungrisdale Common will do much to sooth the troubled mind.

Excellent use is made of the ancient shepherd's path to Skiddaw House in the heart of the northern fells. The return to Keswick takes advantage of the old railroad, now dismantled and converted into a walkway. Once a regular means of communication between Penrith and Cockermouth, the route follows the meandering course carved out by the River Greta

ROUTE DESCRIPTION

Cars may be parked along the road immediately adjacent to Spooney Green Lane, a rough track providing easy and direct access to Latrigg. The track crosses the new A6 Keswick by-pass and winds gently upwards between small plantations of coniferous trees. Avoid paths which go directly up the south facing slopes. They are too steep and make hard work of this easy-going fell.

Instead, work round the western flank of Mallen Dodd before making use of the excellent zig-zag path that branches right, climbing back on itself across the smooth verdant inclination of the Dodd. Seemingly engineered for the sole purpose of assisting aged fell walkers well past their prime, this wide grassy highway leads unerringly to the summit of Latrigg.

Those of a more active persuasion will no doubt be tempted to carry straight on for Skiddaw which beckons invitingly on a clear day. Careful consideration as to whether the ascent of this most popular of routes is to be taken, should depend on the number of other walkers making the pilgrimage.

On the author's last visit to Latrigg in the spring of 1988, the actual top was not immediately obvious; nevertheless the zenith of this splendid little fell is a place to linger and enjoy the southerly aspect over Keswick towards the jaws of Borrowdale. An embankment leads straight across the top where all is grass, interrupted only by a number of isolated trees and old decaying stumps.

At the fence, those who feel time pressing in on them should join the railway track by continuing down the east ridge. The more adventurous will head north, following the fence down to Gale Road and rejoin the Skiddaw path. Immediately after the second stile, take the right fork which crosses Whit Beck and contours round the side of Lonscale Fell.

A surprising amount of height is gained on this track with very little effort as one presses ever onward into the isolated confines of the Glenderaterra Valley. A thin path forks right to circle around the upper reaches of the valley and cross the beck by a wall. Frequented only by sheep, this secluded corner of Lakeland allows a brief interlude for quiet reflection before returning to the traumas of everyday life. After the second gill, leave the upper path to join the old lead mine track alongside the beck.

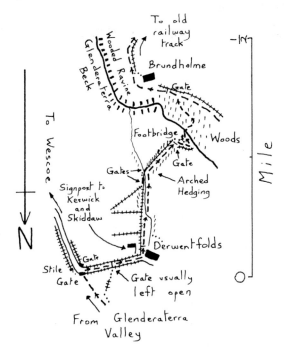

Upon reaching the metalled road, turn right towards Derwentfolds and, using the enlarged map on the previous page, follow a delightful path that· eventually joins the road to Threlkeld.   Heading left, the road beyond Brundholme in 1986 had collapsed and was impassable to motor vehicles. The elements had come out on top in this brief but decisive skirmish with their ancient human adversary.   The humble walker could only stare awestruck at the power of nature, passing on to join the old railway track by means of a wooden bridge. Upon my return to this terrestrial battleground a year later, it was pleasing to note that the local highway authority has seen fit to repair the damaged war zone.

Turning right, make your way back to Keswick along this well maintained route. A series of Skew girder bridges cross the winding Greta each with its own pedestrian walkway.   Leave this track on the right immediately before the old abandoned station to join the lane back to the car. What a splendid climax to a walk of distinction and character.

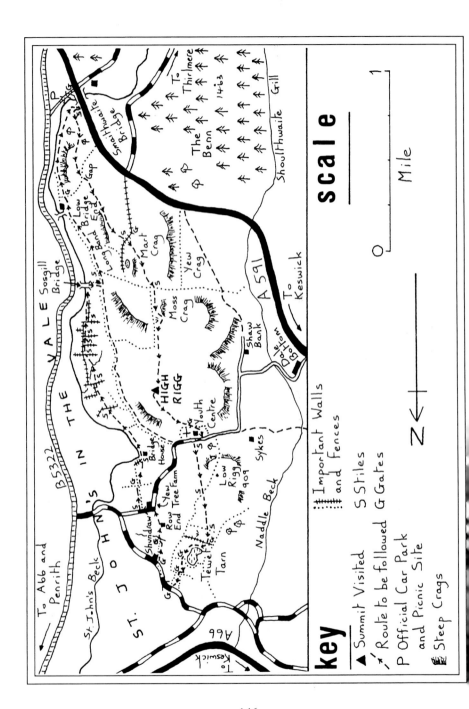

key

▲ Summit Visited

↗ Route to be followed

P Official Car Park and Picnic Site

🌿 Steep Crags

┊┊┊ Important Walls and Fences

S Stiles

G Gates

scale

0 ——————— 1

Mile

N

146

28. NADDLE FELL

Start and Finish: Ample parking is available on an official car park and picnic site 300 yards north of Legburthwaite Church on the left of the B5322.

Summit Visited: High Rigg -1163 feet

Total Height Climbed: 700 feet

Distance Walked: 7.5 miles

Nearest Centre: Keswick

Map Required: Ordnance Survey English Lakes 1:25000, North West area sheet.

INTRODUCTION

Three essential elements that remain uppermost in the minds of the vast majority of fell walkers visiting the Lake District are concerned with ruggedness, height, and a shapely countenance. I am sure that all readers will have their own group of favourites that measure up to at least two of these criteria. I feel equally certain that Naddle Fell will definitely not be among the chosen few.

Such an omission does not mean that this diminutive eminence is unworthy of exploration. What it lacks in altitude and configuration is more than made up for in craggy outcroppings, scattered around the perimeter like a chocolate-chip rock bun. The northern prospect towards Skiddaw and Blencathra is second to none and can be admired from afar. Their crowded thoroughfares, however, are certainly not to be envied.

The most popular motor highway connecting north and south Lakeland passes to the west, yet rarely will a glance be spared for Naddle Fell. To the east, the secluded Vale of St. John provides a short cut through to the A66 but sees little stopping traffic.

The return to Legburthwaite through fenced grassy meadows, enclosed between the steeply shelving flanks of this serene valley, is equally as enjoyable as the attainment of the main objective - High Rigg. Paths are discretely signposted in unobtrusive slate and certainly not overburdened by excessive usage - a firm recommendation in itself.

ROUTE DESCRIPTION

Access to the narrow lane at the northern edge of the car park is gained through a wall gap. Turning left, join the A591 through a gate, then right over Smaithwaite Bridge. Cross a stile and immediately fork left off the main low level track to ascend the open wooded slopes at the southern edge of Naddle Fell.

This section involves the steepest climbing but poses no problems and the rock girt undulating ridge is soon gained without too much effort. Skirting the upper reaches of Wren Crag, a wall is crossed where it enters a craggy depression. A low level route heads round the west side of the facing prominence. The higher level route cuts straight across over the turret and follows Long Band along the top of the ridge on a thin track which improves as the fence is approached.

This sturdy barrier is not shown on my Ordnance Survey map (revised 1981) and is a new addition to the man-made fell furniture. Over the fence stile, the path crosses to the west side of the ridge skirting the splintered ramparts of Mart Crag and descending to a formidable wall effectively dividing the fell into two sectors.

A stile enables progress to be made up a distinct grass track alongside a north pointing arm of wall. Where this turns east down into St. John's-in-the-Vale, continue north towards the upper limit of the ridge known as High Rigg.

The summit cairn is unmistakable, reposing on a table of rock only slightly higher than other surrounding competitors for this prestigious station. On a clear day, the final objective at the northern end of the fell can be seen twinkling in the afternoon sunlight, the eye-catching jewel of Tewet Tarn poses an irresistable attraction.

The most direct descent to St. John's Church follows an easy stroll on grass due north becoming steeper as the pass is approached. Gain the road through a wall gate on a path passing behind the youth centre.

Turning right, a signpost to Tewet Tarn indicates the route over a wall stile across open fields with Low Rigg on the left. Thence the ridge is much lower and less defined. Another wall and fence brings us to the rather disappointing reedy pool which beckoned so invitingly from a distance. More the preserve of cattle who regard human visitors with suspicion, press on to the road which is soon reached after negotiating three walls.

Turn right for the return journey. It is a quarter mile to Shundraw and a signposted path traverses through the fields to Row End. The fell road over to Dale Bottom via the church is soon gained along a rough lane by Yew Tree Farm. Make a left here then right, behind the farm to take a new path alongside a wall through the fields to Bridge House.

Our way lies across the lush meadows adjacent to St. John's Beck. Care is needed along the indistinct route and close attention to the enlarged map on the following page is recommended for this phase which may be a little confusing. A series of stiles eventually leads the resolute traveller to Sosgill Bridge - a superb example of an ancient packhorse bridge still in use across the beck.

Turning west towards High Rigg, join the main track around the base of the fell which leads unerringly back to Smaithwaite Bridge. The only point to note for the future concerns a proposed footpath deviation at Low Bridge End Farm. As the narrow southern entrance to the Vale is approached, the path climbs the precipitous lower wooded slopes of Wren Crag to round the promontory. From the bridge, retrace your outward steps back to the car park.

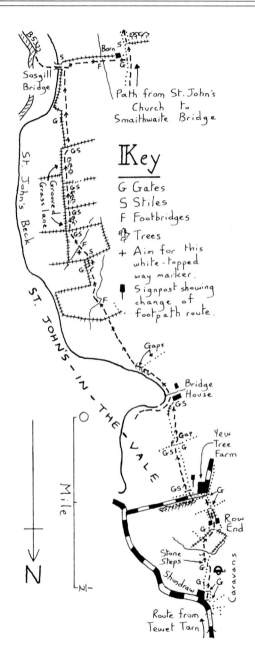

Path from St. John's Church to Smaithwaite Bridge

Key

G Gates
S Stiles
F Footbridges
Trees
+ Aim for this white-topped way marker.
Signpost showing change of footpath route.

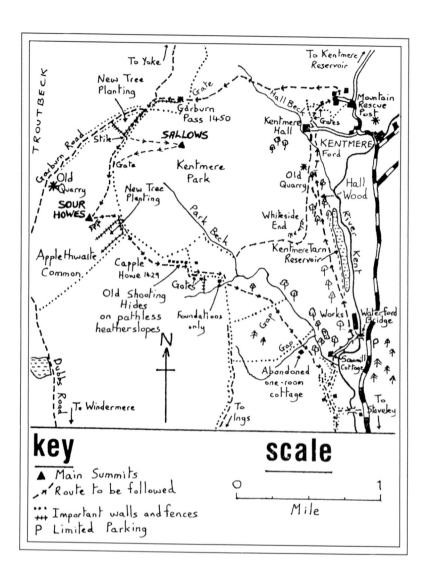

key

▲ Main Summits
↗ Route to be followed
⋮⋮⋮ Important walls and fences
P Limited Parking

scale

0 ——————— 1

Mile

29. KENTMERE PARK

Start and Finish: A small pull-in fifty yards before Waterford Bridge on the right of the Kentmere road heading north.

Summits Visited:	Sallows	-1691 feet
	Sour Howes	-1568 feet

Total Height Climbed: 1100 feet

Distance Walked: 7.5 miles

Nearest Centre: Staveley

Map Required: Ordnance Survey English Lakes 1:25000, South East area sheet.

INTRODUCTION

This walk does not set out to stir the imagination as would a first visit to Mardale Head. Nor does the adrenaline course through pounding veins as with the ascent of Jack's Rake. No - but you are guaranteed the peace and solitude that the more spectacular glories are sadly lacking these days.

The turn-off for Kentmere is easily missed by those intent on seeing 'The Lakes'. Although a glacially carved valley, only a narrow tarn remains of what was once an ancient lake bed extending from Waterford Bridge to Kentmere Hall. Regarded more for its fishing rights than as a beauty spot, this reedy pool is unseen from the valley road. Kentmere is, therefore, regarded as a 'dry' valley. Being a cul-de-sac, it has managed to avoid inclusion on the normal tourist itinerary and is visited purely for its own merits, and by those using it as a stepping stone to the ring of high fells around the classic ice-sculpted dalehead.

A surprisingly isolated valley, I have never encountered more than a handful of visitors in this interesting and geologically varied landscape. Garburn Pass marks the boundary between the high rugged fell country of the Borrowdale Volcanics and the smoother lower level plateau of the Silurian Slates. The craggy nature of the former attracts all fellwalkers hereabouts leaving the latter for the exclusive enjoyment of such as you and I.

ROUTE DESCRIPTION

There is room for two cars only in the small pull-in before Waterford Bridge but it would be a rare occurrence indeed for it to be occupied on your arrival (refer to the enlarged map opposite for the route to Kentmere village). Over the bridge, turn right through the yard of the works to join the old track along the west bank of the River Kent past Kentmere Tarn Reservoir through Hall Wood. Passing through a gate at the lower eastern edge of the wood, the way crosses Hall Beck by a shallow ford and heads straight for Kentmere Hall. Once a 15th-century manor house complete with pele tower for defence against invading brigands, it is now a typical lakeland hill farm.

The signposted path lies through two gates adjacent to one another at the right of the farm buildings. Slanting north west across a walled field, aim for a solid black gate ahead. Then follow the path towards Kentmere village past two cottages. Turn immediately sharp left and join the old pack horse trail connecting the valleys of Kentmere and Troutbeck via the Garburn Pass. Like all such routes designed for the easy passage of man and beast, this follows a pleasant, steady ascent taking advantage of the gentlest gradients and gaining the crest of the pass through a ridge wall gate.

Where the walled Garburn Road begins its descent to the south west, negotiate as best you can an obstructive fence. Do not be deterred however, but follow the narrow gap between fence and wall up to a stile - a new planting of conifers on your right. Here one must decide whether to make acquaintance with the grass bound hillock of Sallows. If a lack of time is your excuse, then continue on the right of the wall picking up a thin path that leads directly onto Sour Howes, a small pile of stones crowning the grassy summit - the final quarter mile bearing right, away from the said wall.

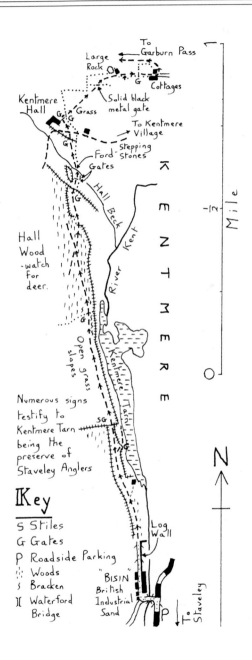

To
Garburn Pass

Large
Rock

Cottages

G

Solid black
metal gate

Kentmere
Hall

G G
Grass

To Kentmere
Village

G

Stepping
Ford Stones
Gates

Hall Beck

K
E
N
T
M
E
R
E

−1⁄2 Mile

Hall
Wood
-watch
for
deer.

River Kent

G

Open grass slopes

0

Kentmere Tarn

Numerous signs
testify to
Kentmere Tarn
being the
preserve of
Staveley Anglers

SG

N

𝕂ey

S Stiles
G Gates
P Roadside Parking
⦙⦙ Woods
∫ Bracken
⟩⟨ Waterford
     Bridge

Log
Wall

"BISIN"
British
Industrial
Sand

P

To Staveley

Returning to the wall, head south over a fence stile adjacent to another new planting of conifers. At the cross wall barrier, one's ingenuity will once again be stretched to negotiate this obstacle with dignity, and the seat of one's pants in tact. Proceed over Capple Howe and down past the old shooting hides - heathery slopes indicating the presence of grouse at one time. Thankfully, we no longer have to witness the sacrifice of these noble birds to the palate of a less enlightened genus.

Follow the wall barring your way to the right where a corner gate provides a way through. This leads to another corner in the wall and the start of a narrow path over the stream across an open plateau south east to a wall gap. A delightful path through the bracken follows Park Beck down to the valley floor. Through the second wall gap, what appears to be an old abandoned shepherd's cottage is worth investigation - the ancient fireplace still remaining intact.

A gate leads into a grassy walled lane which continues down to Ullthwaite Bridge and Browfoot. Take the first branch on the left which becomes a short yet delightful path crossing Park Beck by a footbridge into the grounds of Sawmill Cottage. A path joins the road back to Waterford Bridge and the culmination of a walk to be enjoyed for its solitude amidst the rolling uplands and wooded slopes of Kentmere Park.

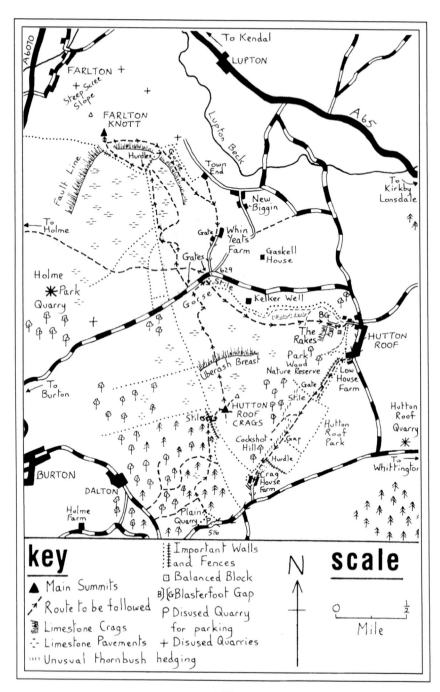

key

▲ Main Summits

Route to be followed

Limestone Crags

Limestone Pavements

Unusual thornbush hedging

Important Walls and Fences

□ Balanced Block

B][G Blasterfoot Gap

P Disused Quarry for parking

+ Disused Quarries

N

scale

0 ——— ½

Mile

30. FARLETON FELL

Start and Finish: Plain Quarry, now disused, provides adequate parking on the Whittington road less than two miles east of Burton.

Summits Visited: Hutton Roof Crags -899 feet
                              Farleton Knott   -853 feet

Total Height Climbed: 800 feet

Distance Walked: 8.5 miles

Nearest Centre: Burton

Maps Required: Ordnance Survey Pathfinder Series 1:25000, Burton (Cumbria), Sheet No. SD 57 **and** Milnthorpe, Sheet No. SD 48/58.

INTRODUCTION

Like a huge primeval leviathan, the whale-backed mass of Farleton Fell presents a solid, unyielding frontage when approached from the north. This bold upthrust of limestone contains a hidden element of Herculean strength that should not be confused with pugnacity.   Along with his craggy entourage, this gentle giant welcomes those who seek to explore a unique and favoured landscape.

Every step of the figure of eight route herein described is a delight to walk, enjoying a variety of scenery that far outweighs the modest altitude involved. The wide expanse of limestone pavement to the north of the cross fell road must be one of the best examples of its kind in the north of England.

It is to be hoped that the large scale quarrying operations taking place on the west side of the fell will be restricted to the lower slopes in order to preserve these very special rock formations. Perhaps those who seek to extract this valuable resource can be persuaded to hide their diligence from those of us who would much prefer to remain in blissful ignorance of their presence.

I always find it pleasantly surprising that such a distinctive ridge has never achieved the degree of popularity that would normally be accorded such a noble mound. Rarely have I encountered other walkers on my travels across the pavements.

ROUTE DESCRIPTION

From the far corner of Plain Quarry, a path heads into the woods alongside a disintegrating wall. Follow this track across Dalton Crags into the upper section of forest. Soon after joining the main forest trail, fork left taking a path which leads straight to the upper eastern edge of the forest. Details of this wooded phase are outlined on the enlarged map section on the opposite page.

Cross the fence stile followed immediately by a wall stile adjacent to a marker cairn. Across the open grass fell, the trig column on Hutton Roof Crags is easily reached. This is the highest point along the ridge and provides a spectacular grandstand view of upland country in three counties - Cumbria, Lancashire and North Yorkshire.

A variety of routes leave the plateau-like summit, Farleton Knott at the far end of the ridge indicating the direction. Paths leading down to the fell road in the depression are sketchy and misleading. A north north westerly bearing can be maintained with confidence in poor visibility but watch out for the abrupt craggy edge of Uberash Breast. A good path, which meanders safely through a tangled web of gorse, emerges as the final descent to the road is approached.

A fence, which has obviously been frequently climbed in the past and now shows signs of imminent collapse, bars progress to the far side of the road.

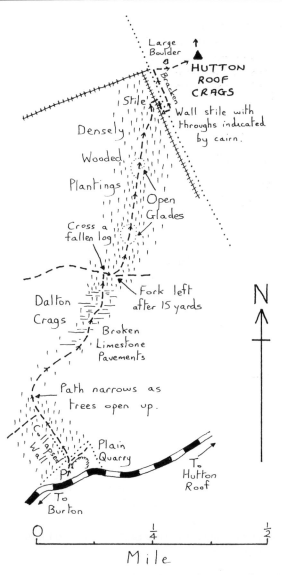

Walkers are asked to respect these barriers which are, after all, constructed for the purpose of restricting sheep - and , of course, restraining impetuous hikers. Turning right, it is but a short distance to the crest where a stile provides an official means of crossing the fence.

Take the bridleway throught the gate opposite for a short distance before joining a more substantial rough track. Follow this to the right branching off near a wall junction to accompany the wall across Newbiggin Crags. Like white horses on a storm-tossed sea, these waves of clint formations invite careful exploration. Where the wall divides, cross a hurdle to follow another onto the lip of a unique geological fault line which forms a collar of limestone crag around the neck of our dormant gargantuan. A simple stroll across the col gives access to his bald dome.

Leaving the summit, return to the col and follow the fault line eastwards round to cross another hurdle. The path descends gently through gorse before joining the upcoming bridleway from Town End. Passing through the yard of Whin (Wind on the O.S. map) Yeats Farm, rejoin the fell road and return to the crest.

Negotiate the stile signposted to Hutton Roof for the second time and tread a delightful trail around the lower reaches of Hutton Roof Crags. The original path appears to have fallen into disuse in favour of the higher route. It descends to Hutton Roof village by way of a climbers' playground called The Rakes and through the defiantly named Blasterfoot Gap. Here also are to be found some smaller yet no less distinctive angular pavements supported by simple limestone crags which can be enjoyed by anyone - provided of course that the necessary care is exercised when handling bare rock. Audacious desperados will not doubt be tempted to challenge the balancing properties of the acrobatic boulder precariously perched above the village.

Do not be attracted by the red herring of a footpath heading right when the lower wall is reached. Instead, go left to gain the village main street. After walking the length of the picturesque settlement, bear right, through Low House Farm yard. Take the footpath through the fields beginning with a gate offset from the main farm track. A series of stiles and gates eventually leads through Crag House Farm to the Burton road and Plain Quarry is soon reached after a simple stroll.

The gradients involved on this walk are barely noticeable but the distance should not be underestimated. For those who enjoy the quiet contrasts of an everchanging landscape amidst the unique rock formations characteristic of limestone country, this walk is a must.

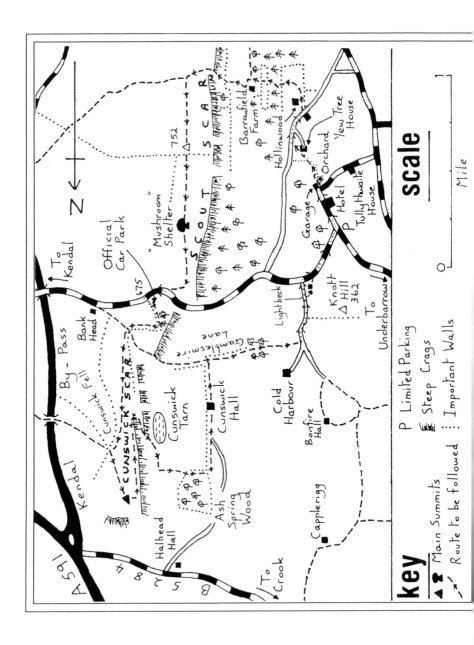

key

▲☘ Main Summits
--- Route to be followed

P Limited Parking
☘ Steep Crags
⋮ Important Walls

scale

0 _____ 1

Mile

31. ALONG THE SCARS

Start and Finish: The road junction where Thorns Lane joins the Kendal to Underbarrow road at grid reference 474919.

Summits Visited:	Scout Scar	-764 feet
	Cunswick Scar	-679 feet

Total Height Climbed: 750 feet

Distance Walked: 7.5 miles

Nearest Centre: Kendal

Map Required: Ordnance Survey English Lakes 1:25000, South East area sheet.

INTRODUCTION

Immediately to the west of Kendal, a spectacular north - south escarpment of limestone cliffs separates the Lyth and Kent valleys. The usual line of approach is from Kendal, which lies just outside the boundaries of the National Park, and remains a firm favourite with the citizens of this illustrious gateway to the South Lakes. Access from the east provides a gradual and easy ascent barely two miles from the town centre. It does, however, fail to give sufficient opportunity for walkers to fully appreciate the sculpturing of these celebrated limestone scars. It is in fact possible to walk the upper edge without any knowledge of the precipitous bluffs so close at hand.

Only when approaching from the west is one able to experience the full majesty along the two fault lines - Cunswick being oddly set back from its more popular neighbour, Scout. A far more important reason for a western approach, however, is that one is far less likely to encounter other explorers. The exception, of course, is along the south scar where 'mushroom' seekers cannot be avoided, this being the local name for the distinctive shelter adorning the summit of Scout Scar.

The route herein described is an interesting test in route selection, this being a relatively unfrequented circuit with paths that are sketchy and overgrown. As a test of stamina and endurance, however, it does not quite rank with the Gables and Scafells of this world. My young son was more than capable of negotiating the route - with a little help from his dad, of course.

ROUTE DESCRIPTION

Parking is available on the wide grass verge adjacent to the narrow Thorns Lane which branches from the Underbarrow road. Details of this initial wooded phase are illustrated on the enlarged map opposite. Walk down past the hotel to a small private garage where the lane bends sharply to the west. The path follows a stone wall on the right of the garage next to an orchard. It is overgrown with nettles so ladies are advised to wear trousers or use a walking stick to attack them. After struggling through the initial 100 yards of jungle, the path widens to negotiate a cross wall stile then continues behind Yew Tree House to join a narrow back lane.

Follow this past Garthrow until a track on the left indicates the access road to Hollinwood. When the path fades after passing to the right of this settlement, bear left up to a gate in the wall enclosing Barrowfield Lot conifer plantation. A distinct path meanders through this eerie twilight world which can only be experienced in such surroundings, crossing a rough forest road and continuing ahead to a boundary wall. Avoid all red herrings leading right or left. At the edge of the wood look for a stile into another smaller wood across the opposite side of the open field.

After this wood, we arrive - hopefully - at Barrowfield. Make your way through the farmyard and across the open fields up to a gate giving access to the lower wooded slopes of Scout Scar, the upper edge of which is easily reached on a good path. Once the crest is gained, continue east for 100 yards

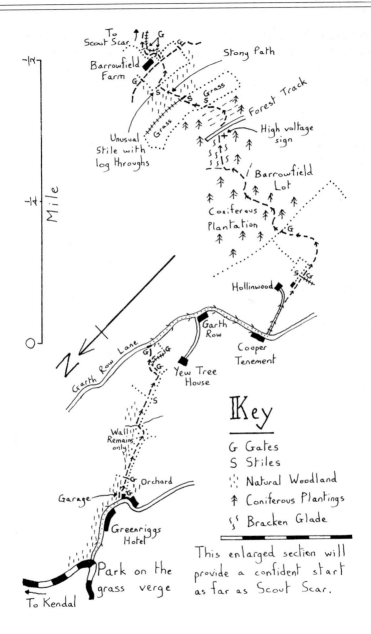

Key

G Gates
S Stiles
: Natural Woodland
↑ Coniferous Plantings
₅₅ Bracken Glade

This enlarged section will provide a confident start as far as Scout Scar.

167

until the ridge proper can be followed northwards. The trig column is easily missed lying close to the wall which crosses the Scar running east to west. Passing through a gap, it is but an easy stroll to the 'mushroom' shelter which is set back from the escarpment rim.

The domed cover of this man-made edifice contains an excellent viewfinder and visual indicator of all the upland country in sight. Having identified all your past conquests and made surreptitious plans for future expeditions, continue northwards until the path makes a sharp turn to the right. The Underbarrow road which takes advantage of the depression between the two Scars is soon gained via a stile.

Turning right towards Kendal, walk as far as the main car park on the left, at the rear of which a path enters a small wood past a communications mast. At the north corner of the wood a stile gives access to a field. Follow the wall around to cross Gamblesmire Lane, making use of the map below.

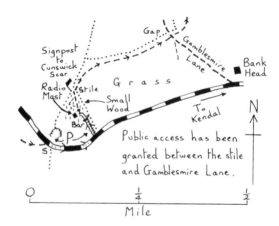

This old, rough fell road is the only other line of communication across the Scars. Our way lies northwards between a narrow walled causeway across Cunswick Fell bearing right to join the main path from Kendal. Make a left across open grass pasture to gain the large white cairn surmounting the apex of Cunswick Scar.

Returning along the edge of the Scar, there appears to be no safe descent of the vertical escarpment plunging into the woods below. Do not despair, however, a delectable path soon emerges after a quarter mile leading one safely and easily down to the lower slopes. At the bottom, through a stile, the way lies straight across an open field into Ash Spring Wood. The path follows the wall along the southern edge. Turn left immediately out of the wood and follow the wall - no visible path - joining the access road to Cunswick Hall.

After discovering the correct route through the maze of farm buildings, continue south to join Gamblesmire Lane. Turning right, follow it down through a wood. The lower section of the lane is much overgrown, narrowing between hedges before reaching a metalled farm road. Take a left here to eventually join the Underbarrow road and a right at Lightbeck to lead you back to the car - an interesting circuit if ever there was one, and a challenge to all those who enjoy testing their map reading abilities.

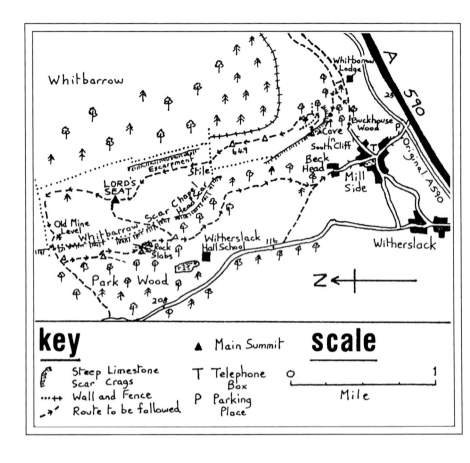

Whitbarrow

Whitbarrow Lodge

A 590

25

Buckhouse Wood

Cave in South Cliff

P

T

Beck Head

Mill Side

Original A590

Escarpment

649

Stile

LORD'S SEAT

Scar Chapel Head Scar

Witherslack

Old Mine Level

Whitbarrow

Witherslack Hall School

116

Rock Slabs

Park Wood

208

Z ←

170

32. WHITBARROW SCAR

Start and Finish: Limited parking is available where the Mill Side road widens at its junction with the old A590.

Summit Visited: Lord's Seat -706 feet

Total Height Climbed: 750 feet

Distance Walked: 6.5 miles

Nearest Centre: Levens Village

Map Required: Ordnance Survey Pathfinder Series 1:25000, Milnthorpe, Sheet No. SD 48/58.

INTRODUCTION

An enormous wedge of limestone thrusting out onto the flats of the Kent estuary, Whitbarrow issues its challenge to the passing motorist. The fell is often overlooked by those hurrying to sample the more exotic attractions in the heart of the Lake District. Only the discerning few bother to avail themselves of the hidden charms around this lonely outpost of Lakeland.

Whitbarrow's mellow east flank overlooks the lush pastures of the Lyth Valley - renowned for the abundance and quality of its damson harvest in late summer. Like a Jekyll and Hyde character, this soft, easy-going side to the fell's nature can be austere and unforgiving to those who fail to show true respect. Nevertheless, Whitbarrow remains a choice item among the limestone delicacies on offer in south Cumbria.

Viewed from the sylvan seclusion of the Witherslack Valley, the battlemented ramparts of the Scar edge stretch away into the distance. The commanding presence of this solid wall of limestone dominates the eastern perimeter of the hidden dale and is sufficient to generate a plethora of excitement difficult to contain.

Rarely visited, the peaceful qualities of the valley are reason enough for looking no further. Rescued from a bygone age when life moved at a more leisurely pace, Witherslack exists in a vacuum of the mind. The rush and bustle of the outside world has no place here.

The variety of scenery experienced on this walk by far outweighs the modest effort entailed in its ascent - the delightful, expansive ridge contrasting sharply with the dense valley woodland. The old limestone quarry on the south east flank presents a formidable barrier which might well discourage the faint hearted approaching from Levens. No need to despair, however. The ridge is easily gained from Mill Side at its southern edge.

ROUTE DESCRIPTION

A quarter mile walk up from the old A590 brings us to the centre of the hamlet of Mill Side. The new road is straighter and wider, built for the sole purpose of improving communications with south west Cumbria. Take the right fork by the telephone box and strike up the farm road towards Buckhouse Wood.

Here the road becomes rougher but levels out to circle the lower slopes of the Scar. Fifty yards after the entrance to Whitbarrow Lodge comes in sight, take a narrow path slanting left through the trees. Go left again at a major forest trail which narrows on the gradual climb up to the base of the south cliff. This section involves a considerable amount of bending to avoid overhanging branches placed at a somewhat inconvenient height for six footers such as myself. A small cave in the rock face provides welcome shelter in poor conditions but can only be reached after negotiating an awkward fallen tree. Some difficulty might well be experienced in retaining one's dignity when tackling this obstacle.

After skirting the cliff, the trees thin out and the path forks. Take the high route which snakes up onto the crag top. Bear right and follow a wall round into more trees passing through a gap and up onto the ridge proper. The ridge can be gained more directly by continuing on the lower first path to a distinct stream and joining an upper path which turns sharp left, climbing up to the wall gap. The initial confusion of this steep section at the start of the walk should be eliminated using the large scale map section below.

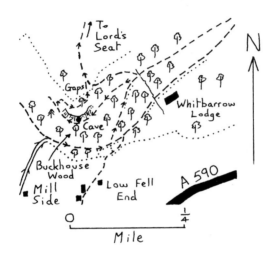

Looking north along the ridge, Lord's Seat dominates the skyline - a noble aristocrat commanding all lesser heights around. The enjoyable summit walk follows a central course with a coniferous plantation on the right and the hidden precipice of the Scar to the left.

Crossing a wall by a stile, one enters a conservation area under the control of the Lake District Naturalists' Trust. Your co-operation in helping to promote this nature reserve by keeping to the paths would be much appreciated. After following a disintegrating limestone escarpment for half a mile on your right, move left away from the scarp to gain the highest point and its stately pinnacle via a short embankment.

From Lord's Seat, a way down to the valley is available to the south west where a distinct path soon emerges as the scar edge wall is approached.

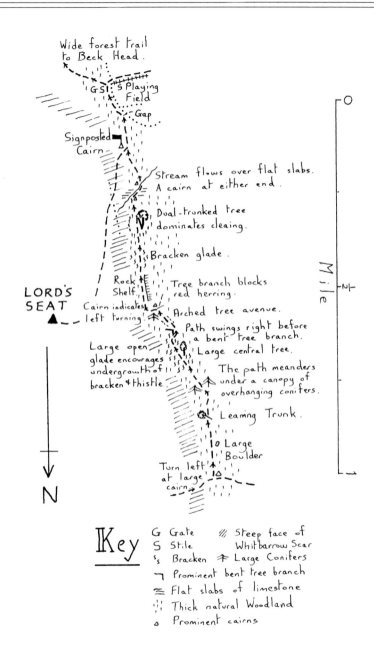

Wide forest trail
to Beck Head.

G S1   S Playing
Field
Gap

Signposted
Cairn

Stream flows over flat slabs.
A cairn at either end.

Dual-trunked tree
dominates clearing.

Bracken glade.

Rock
Shelf

Tree branch blocks
red herring.

LORD'S
SEAT

Cairn indicates
left turning!

Arched tree avenue.

Path swings right before
a bent tree branch.

Large open
glade encourages
undergrowth of
bracken + thistle

Large central tree.

The path meanders
under a canopy of
overhanging conifers.

Leaning Trunk.

Large
Boulder

Turn left
at large
cairn

N

Mile

O

½

1

Key

G	Gate	/// Steep face of
S	Stile	Whitbarrow Scar
ˢₛ	Bracken	🌲 Large Conifers
	⌐	Prominent bent tree branch
	≈	Flat slabs of limestone
	⋮⋮	Thick natural Woodland
	o	Prominent cairns

Otherwise, continue along the ridge until a cross fell wall is reached. Turning west, the path leads down past an old mine level. At the northern end of Whitbarrow Scar, the path drops quite steeply over loose scree into dense woodland. September marks the beginning of the game shooting season which extends through the autumn until January. As these woods are the home of deer and pheasant, a warning must obviously be issued.

A left hand cairn indicates the start of a narrow, yet interesting, trail winding through the trees following the base of the Scar. A second important cairn points to a left fork which should be taken in preference to the red herring continuing straight ahead. The path becomes indistinct when a stream is reached flowing across flat rock slabs. Two cairns show the way. Detailed instructions for negotiating this interesting mile through the woods are provided on the enlarged map on the opposite page.

After joining the main path off the Scar at a large signposted cairn, continue past the playing fields used by the boys of Witherslack Hall School. The forest trail winds through the trees until the bridleway from the valley road is joined. This track soon becomes a metalled highway at the tiny settlement of Beck Head where a sub-terranian stream characteristic of limestone country debouches from the base of a low crag and wends its merry way down to feed the reservoir at Mill Side. The short walk back to this hamlet completes a splendid ramble of variety and contrasting scenic beauty.

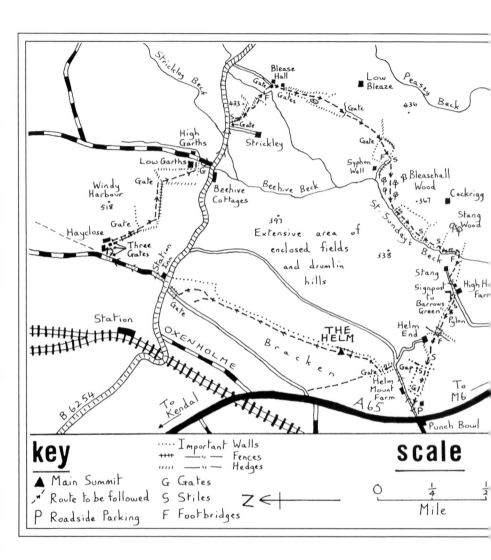

Strickley Beck

Blease Hall

Low Bleaze

Peasey Beck

436

Gate

Gates

Gate

433

Gate

High Garths

Gate

Strickley

Low Garths

Gate

Windy Harbour

518

Gate

Hayclose

Three Gates

Beehive Cottages

Beehive Beck

Syphon Well

Bleasehall Wood

·367

Cockrigg

Stang Wood

Extensive area of enclosed fields and drumlin hills

397

St. Sunday's Beck

338

Stang

Signpost To Barrows Green

High H Farm

Pylon

Station Inn

Gate

Station

OXENHOLME

Bracken

THE HELM

Helm End

Helm Mount Farm

Gate

Gap

B 6254

To Kendal

A 65

Punch Bowl

To M6

key

···· Important Walls
++++ —— Fences
'''' — '' — Hedges

▲ Main Summit
,×' Route to be followed
P Roadside Parking

G Gates
S Stiles
F Footbridges

Z ←

scale

0   ¼   ½
Mile

176

33. BEYOND THE HELM

Start and Finish: Turn right off the A65 at Barrow's Green opposite the Punch Bowl Inn and park on the grass verge of this narrow lane.

Summit Visited: The Helm   -607 feet

Total Height Climbed: 600 feet

Distance Walked: 5.5 miles

Nearest Centre: Oxenholme

Maps Required: Ordnance Survey English Lakes 1:25000, South East area sheet **and** Ordnance Survey Pathfinder Series 1:25000, Milnthorpe, Sheet No. SD 48/58.

INTRODUCTION

The elongated wedge of roughly-hewn Silurian gritstone which stands guard over the settlement of Oxenholme must be the easiest summit to reach in the district. Its attainment does, however, provide one of the finest local views across the Kent valley towards Kendal. A walk along the crest gives the impression of a promenade that one would expect to encounter in the higher fells. As such it can be enjoyed by any person in reasonable health, entailing little effort for the benefits gained.

The compact nature of The Helm makes it an ideal stroll for those who are based in Kendal and only have a few hours to spare. After traversing the full length of the ridge, a return along the lane on the Oxenholme side connecting the A65 with the B6254 makes an excellent outing for a fine summer's evening.

Those who would prefer a more extended expedition are equally well catered for, although the walk herein described is more akin to a ramble and can in no way be regarded as a fell walk once The Helm is left behind. The only rocks to be encountered are those making up the vast mileage of stone walling in the vicinity.

Few people obviously bother to tread the rights-of-way in this area as the paths are overgrown and barely discernible along much of the route. Apart from the expected encounters on The Helm, I met nobody and have every intention to seek out more of these neglected backwaters that have sadly fallen into disuse. I recommend others to make their acquaintance and thus take advantage of pathways along which the general public are fully entitled to walk. The enclosed farmland surmounts a deluge of small, whale-backed hillocks called drumlins. These distinctive features of glacial depostion are referred to as 'a basket of eggs' topography, elongated in a north east to south west direction which indicates the direction of ice movement.

ROUTE DESCRIPTION

After walking to the top of the metalled access lane past Helm Mount Farm, turn left along a grass track for no more than 100 yards. Immediately through the gate, take a right through the lower gorse bushes following the wall up a fairly steep but short open slope onto the summit of The Helm.

The trig column is gained before we have had a chance to get started and cannot, therefore, be regarded as the prime objective as is usually the case on these walks. Continue on the left of the ridge wall following the path down to the fell road contouring the lower slopes. The Station Hotel is quickly reached after passing through the road gate. No loitering here, you haven't earned it yet. Instead, cross the B6254 and walk up the opposite lane for a half mile to Hayclose.

A wooden gate on the right immediately before the cluster of farm buildings gives access to the bridleway. This track indicates the way through two further gates and the farmyard, thence across a field adjacent to a fence. After another gate, the track fades out as a fence is approached. Bear left and follow this fence to another gate on the right. A diagonal crossing of the field leads to Low Garths farmyard and a narrow lane. Walk south to the B6254 and turn left along this road as far as the rough farm track to Strickley which is on the right.

Immediately beyond is a gate which indicates a new start to the right-of-way over the crest of a drumlin and down to Blease Hall. Cross a stile on the left immediately after this gate being careful to avoid touching the electric cow barrier. Turn left through the hedge gap to accompany it over the hill and down to cross St. Sunday's Beck by a decaying footbridge. Across the field, a gate gives access to the farm.

Make your way through the conglomeration of farm buildings that comprise Blease Hall - the actual domicile being quite easy to identify - to emerge through a double gate barrier at its southern extremity into a rough walled lane. The track opens out into a field circling the left side of a pond then keeps close to the right hedge boundary as far as another gate. The way continues along the right side of a ditch to pass through a wall gap. Cross the field to a fence/wall junction noting the square syphon well on your right in an adjoining field.

A footbridge and stile give access to Bleasehall Wood and another 'shocking' barrier, although this one can be stepped over quite easily without enhancing one's electrifying personality. A grass track leads to a wall stile alongside St. Sunday Beck. Follow this by a wall on your right over two further stiles before crossing it via a footbridge just beyond Stang. A path heads north west across open ground to join a metalled lane by a cottage.

Turn left along this lane as far as the second signpost pointing the way to Barrows Green opposite High House Farm. Cross the field alongside the wall passing to the right of an electric pylon. Then over the rise and down the facing slope through a hedged causeway - beware of a single strand of barbed wire. Cross a concrete stream bridge continuing the roller coaster past Helm End to a stile hidden in a hedge. Bear left across the field to its corner and over another stile in a wall (this is to the left of an obvious gap which is not a right-of-way).

A steep ascent of this last field accompanying a wall/fence descends to a gate and thence down to the outgoing lane. Turn left back to the car and the chance of a welcome beverage at the Punch Bowl.

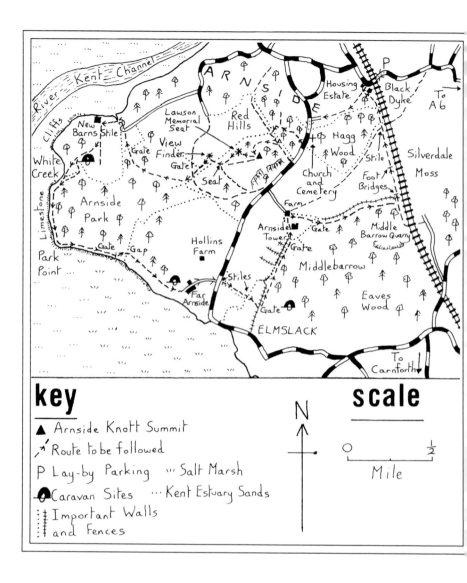

key

▲ Arnside Knott Summit
↗ Route to be followed
P Lay-by Parking   ʷ Salt Marsh
⬤ Caravan Sites   ⋯ Kent Estuary Sands
⫶ Important Walls
⫶ and Fences

scale

N

0 ——— ½

Mile

34. ARNSIDE KNOTT

Start and Finish: Approaching from the east, a lay-by provides good parking on the right one hunderd yards before the Black Dyke railway crossing.

Summit Visited: Arnside Knott   -521 feet

Total Height Climbed: 550 feet

Distance Walked: 6.5 miles

Nearest Centre: Arnside

Map Required: Ordnance Survey Pathfinder Series 1:25000, Grange over Sands, Sheet No. SD 37/47.

INTRODUCTION

Overlooking the estuary of the River Kent, this modest outcrop of limestone enables young and old alike to sharpen their claws without too much effort. My nine year old son completed the circuit in fine form with no complaints other than his dad's choice of soup for lunch.

More akin to a ramble than an actual fell walk, this wooded enclave forms part of the Silverdale/Arnside Area of Outstanding Natural Beauty. Smaller than a national park but with similar conservation aims, this Lilliputian landscape encompasses mixed woodland amidst the emergent silvery jewelled limestone substratum. Extending southwards from White Creek, I invite readers to share with me the bewitching experience of sampling one of the most exquisite low level paths I have ever had the pleasure of treading. It follows a delicate, meandering trail around the edge of Arnside Park, above sea-weathered ramparts of limestone cliff.

Being a natural focus for walkers, the upper environs of the Knott have an abundance of paths and are likely to be fairly well populated on any fine weekend in the year. Do not be put off, however; this is a walk of exceptional merit to be undertaken when time is short or poor weather prevents a more extended expedition. On this occasion, for once, the objective is not to escape, just to relish the display of unrivalled scenery that constitutes the essential elements of all that is best in this area of outstanding natural beauty.

ROUTE DESCRIPTION

From the Black Dyke lay-by, cross the railway line taking the path which follows the north edge of Hagg Wood. This passes along the back gardens of bungalows on the Plantation Avenue housing estate. At the upper end, a new residential development has resulted in an official detour for the present right of way.

On this occasion, the change of route causes no inconvenience returning to its original course by joining Spinney Lane. However, those of us who often frequent the by-ways of rural England sometimes encounter unwarranted barriers to progress along designated rights of way. Such obstructions are thankfully few and far between these days due to the tenacious efforts of groups such as the Ramblers' Association.

Turn left into Silverdale Road past the cemetery until the entrance to Red Hills Wood is reached. This is a relatively recent orientation not marked on current Ordnance Survey maps but full details can be found on the enlarged map opposite. Bear up left to a wall junction with a double stile. Turn left after passing through the wall stile and move down to an indistinct right turn marked by a prominent cairn.

The path bears left away from the ridge wall to wind between open trees onto the summit of Arnside Knott. Barely over 500 feet above sea level, we are still below the tree line with a consequent restriction in views. A short walk to the west provides a more open aspect across the Kent estuary from the relative comfort of the Lawson memorial seat.

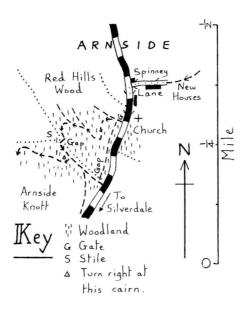

Continue along the ridge past the 'giraffe' - an unusual interlacing of two separate trees - towards the open depression. Pass straight across, through a thicket, keeping right onto the western extremity where a more worthy viewpoint is provided. A Don Ainslie engraving on metal plates allows instant identification of all landmarks in sight from this lofty perch.

From here, the path drops sharply alongside a neglected wall into dense woodland to join the main bridleway from Arnside around the Knott. Turning left, follow it until a signpost to White Creek is reached. A right turn here should bring you to the gate at the northern edge of Copridding Wood, provided all red herrings on either side are resisted. To avoid getting lost, use the second small map on the following page to help you through the woods. Cross the open field through an old kissing gate to gain the road to New Barns.

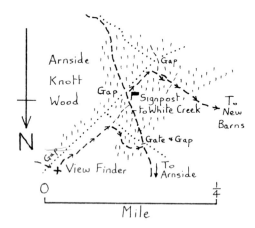

From here, a signpost to Far Arnside points the way. Fork right off the farm track through a caravan site and so to White Creek. Aptly named on account of its sea-washed pebble beach, this perfectly shaped eliptical bay provides a rare opportunity to aquaint one's self with the secret charms of this delightful corner of Eden. Time has lost its meaning in this enchanting cove and an irresistable urge to linger should be satisfied.

The enchantment is maintained on the beautiful walk around the headland of Park Point to Far Arnside. Passing through another caravan site, the Silverdale Road is crossed and a path taken through the fields. At the far side of the shallow dry valley, turn left through a gate and head north along an old rough lane to Arnside Tower. This medieval pele tower once protected the valley from marauding Celtic invaders but is now a dangerous ruin that should be approached with care.

Do not enter the Tower farmyard. Instead, go right into Middlebarrow Wood through a broken gate, following its perimeter round to the railway. Turning left, accompany the railway across a series of footbridges and stiles in a direct line back to Black Dyke.

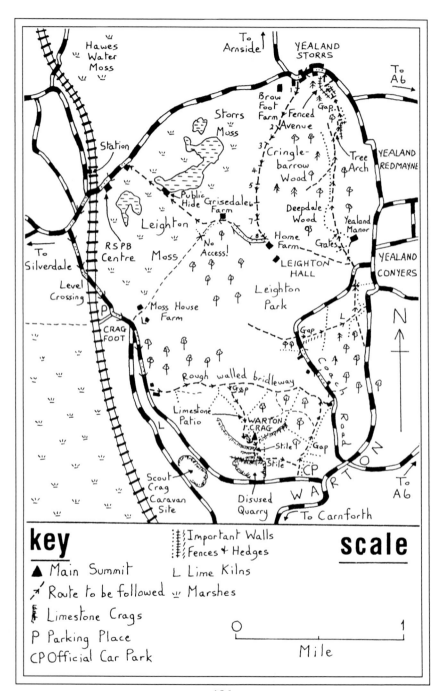

key

▲ Main Summit

Route to be followed

Limestone Crags

P Parking Place

CP Official Car Park

Important Walls

Fences & Hedges

L Lime Kilns

Marshes

scale

0 —————————— 1

Mile

35. LEIGHTON PARK

Start and Finish: Ample parking is available along the side lane 200 yards on the left beyond the hamlet of Crag Foot on the way to Silverdale.

Summit Visited: Warton Crag   -534 feet

Total Height Climbed: 750 feet

Distance Walked: 8.5 miles

Nearest Centre: Warton

Maps Required: Ordnance Survey Pathfinder Series 1:25000, Grange over Sands, Sheet No. SD 37/47 **and** Burton (Cumbria), Sheet No. SD 57.

INTRODUCTION

The high point of this walk in both senses of the word is the ascent of Warton Crag. Steadfast followers of these walks who are relishing the aesthetic appreciation of distinctive fell summits may well feel a little let down if their approach is from the north. Blending into the rolling woodland scenery that is characteristic of the countryside to the south of Kendal, the Crag makes no extrovert pretentions from this angle.

From Morecambe, the true grandeur of the fell captures the eye magnificently, presenting a shapely profile to the Bay. It has the unmistakable appearance of a home-made gateau complete with layers of creamy filling. The insatiable appetite of industry has, however, resulted in a mammoth - sized bite of tasty limestone being snaffled from the south flank. Thankfully, these activities have moved on to pastures new. The scars however, still remain.

Much of the walk beyond Warton Crag proceeds through a variety of wooded tracts that need care in view of the numerous paths therein. Such is the extensive nature of this arboreal kingdom that small herds of deer are able to thrive.

I encountered these shy creatures having at one point found myself wandering in circles in Cringlebarrow Wood. Having attempted a short cut not shown on the Ordnance Survey map, I had to retrace my steps for a considerable distance before regaining the correct path. Readers are encouraged to follow the route herein described along recognised rights-of-way if they are to avoid the author's miscalculations.

ROUTE DESCRIPTION

Returning to Crag Foot, take the upper road circling the fell for a half mile until a bridleway to Coach Road is reached. Turn left and follow this through the lower woodland as far as an official gap on the right just beyond the last in-take wall. Pass through and accompany a delightful trail across the open fell ignoring paths branching left.

A brief visit to the miniature limestone patio on the right of the path is well worth ten minutes of anybody's time. Cross the fell wall and make a leisurely ascent across the crags up onto the plateau-like summit.

The upper tier of limestone forms a natural defensive bulwark and was adopted as a fortification by the ancients who inhabited this area in the distant past. Present day occupants are much more peaceable and seek only to enjoy the expansive seascape to the south across Morecambe Bay. On a clear day - and with a little imagination - I can just make out my own humble residence beyond Hunting Hill at Crag Bank. The aspect to the north is restricted by a sylvan thatch of woodland covering most of the summit area.

Leave the top to follow the cross summit wall east for about twenty yards before striking down the open slope to descend the first rock step over a stile. Two further steps continue the declevity as far as a strong fence - an essential barrier to fatal progress over the abrupt quarry edge.

Head left over a stile to descend a slanting bench of limestone to an in-take wall hidden until the last minute by small trees. Turn left to follow the wall through Potts Wood. Various direction arrows provide an obvious indication of the route to the main bridlepath gained through a wall gap. Descend to Coach Road, then go left for a half mile until a gap stile abutting a field gate is reached opposite a rough lane. The way lies east through the fields past an old lime kiln. Watch for another gap stile in a wall on your right. Our way lies left here along a corridor between trees and a high wall.

After crossing a fence stile, join the Yealand Conyers road. Descend right for 100 yards before passing through another stile to gain the path heading north through Deepdale Wood. Stick to the main track past Yealand Manor keeping in a northerly direction all the time into Cringlebarrow Wood.

At the end of a straight section on the east side, the path forks. Take the right prong heading down under an unusual ivy and holly arch of branches and passing an open fenced field. The final wooded phase of the walk terminates with a fenced, grassy avenue between new plantings of conifers. Keep straight ahead along this verdant sward to join the road. Use the large scale map on the following page to guide you through this confusing woodland tract.

Take a left through the hamlet of Yealand Storrs until one of the new abbreviated footpath signs is reached. A diminutive wicket gate in a high wall gives access to the path making for Home Farm. Keep a count of the eight field gates - open or closed - that need to be passed through before the road to Grisedale Farm is gained. Head right to pass by the farm.

From here it is less than a mile back to Crag Foot but the field path lies across private land and is barred to walkers. A detour right must, therefore, be taken across the Leighton Moss causeway. This does have the advantage of traversing a unique bird sanctuary run by the Royal Society for the Protection of Birds. A public hide, half way along the causeway, provides

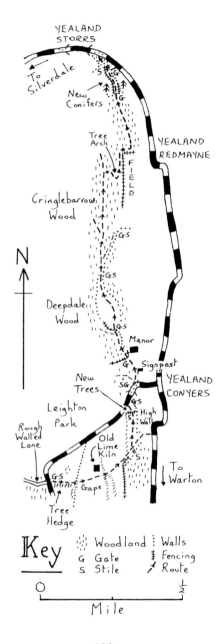

YEALAND
STORRS

To
Silverdale

New
Conifers

Tree
Arch

YEALAND
REDMAYNE

F
I
E
L
D

Cringlebarrow
Wood

GS

N

GS

Deepdale
Wood

GS

Manor

Signpost

G

New
Trees

SG

YEALAND
CONYERS

GS

Leighton
Park

High
Wall

Rough
Walled
Lane

Old
Lime
Kiln

S

To
Warton

GS

Gaps

Tree
Hedge

Key

Woodland
G Gate
S Stile

Walls
Fencing
Route

0   ½

Mile

190

a rare opportunity to observe more unusual species of birds in a natural and protected environment.

Immediately after the visitor centre, turn left into a country lane. Two further lefts and a little over a mile of road walking returns us to the car - the culmination of a fine walk encompassing all manner of rural scenery.